GETTING PAST STUCK

"Out of the Mud—FOREVER!"

By Terence B. Lester

GETTING PAST STUCK
© 2012 by Terence B. Lester
Printed by U-Turn Books, LLC.

Scripture taken from the Holy Bible, New International Version®. Copyright © 1973, 1978, 1984 International Bible Society. Used by permission of Zondervan. All rights reserved.

Scripture quotations marked NKJV™ are taken from the New King James Version®. Copyright © 1982 by Thomas Nelson, Inc. Used by permission. All rights reserved.

ISBN-978-0-615-60698-9

Printed in the United States of America

Table of Contents

Dedication

*I dedicate this book to my beautiful wife, **Cecilia**, who is my best friend and my constant support. With similar passion, I humbly acknowledge our daughter, **Zion Joy Lester**, and our son, **Terence B. Lester II**, who encourages me every day of my life. All three of you have a special place in my heart.*

Additionally, this book is dedicated to every person who feels defeated and deflated. May God's grace become enough for you wherever you are!

Acknowledgements

My whole being is filled with praise for the many individuals who have blessed my life. Before all else, I dedicate this book to *God*. Without His Son Jesus in my life, none of this would be possible. I love Him for giving me undeserved grace and unmerited favor.

A special thank you has been earned by one of the most supportive people in my life, my wife, *Cecilia L. Lester*. If called upon to compare you with an element, I'd relate you to the wind. Your support has been the wind beneath my wings. I love you.

To the biological as well as extended family God has given to me, thanks for the constant prayers and support you give to *Cecilia*, *Zion*, *Terence II*, and me.

To my mother, *Connie Walker*, thanks for always pushing *Cecilia* and me to be the best we can be. Thank you as well for being a mother who believes in her son.

To my sister *Ashley Lester* and my nephew *Carmelo O'Neal*, I love you both with all my heart.

To *Harvey Strickland III*, thank you for being a friend, brother, and an encourager in my life.

Finally, I would like to acknowledge the counselors I have worked with, *Gary Fox, Rick Bemis*, and *Dr. Bruce Atkinson* for how they helped me to process ideas and past experiences, and to understand the power of perception.

Foreword

When I think of the word "stuck," the first thing that comes to mind is chewing gum. We have all had the experience of our shoes being plastered with gum from accidentally stepping on gum left on the ground by someone else. We search for the closest object we can find to remove the feeling of being stuck: a piece of cardboard, a sheet of paper, even the curb.

In fact, having gum on the bottom of your shoe is one of the most irritating feelings in the world. Somehow, it creates a feeling of not being able to get out of what's trying to hold you down. Even though we eventually get rid of the gum, that same feeling holds true when our lives somehow get tangled up in depression, bad decisions, unexpected events, disappointment, or failure. We become stuck in a web of irritation and, if not careful, we end up using the wrong objects that will keep us stuck there for a long time. It is extremely important that we have wisdom, principles, and people around us when our lives seem stuck.

As the wife of Terence Lester, I have watched him grow beyond measure. In this book, he has outlined many principles and techniques to aid you as you press to get past failure, failed relationships, despair, depression, unforeseen circumstances, or current opposition, internal or external. All these categories can make us feel stuck and powerless to move forward. His principles have stayed with me throughout the years, especially when my life feels like a big shoe and my problems feel like the gum that have me stuck. He has taught me that our faith plays a very intricate role in our ability to move forward after we have encountered adversity. Our faith in God empowers us to move forward even when ALL odds seem stacked against us. I have learned that when you come to that point, you have to make up your mind that you don't want to stay there and that you have to move forward. This book teaches just that. While living our lives, we hit bumps in the road and we must be prepared to move forward after we encounter them. If not, they will take us out.

It takes a lot for people to admit that they are STUCK. After reading this book, you will be able to recognize when you are coming to the point where you feel STUCK and need help, and also know what tools to use to help you get past stuck. Not only is this book an easy read, but it is practical and relevant for real life situations.

Terence has made a choice to overcome adversity and life's challenges by relying on his faith. James 2:20 states, "But do you want to know, O foolish man, that faith without works is dead? (NKJV)" Learning how to move past the challenges and obstacles in life can be challenging, but choosing to overcome trials can catapult you to your destiny. My husband has done an excellent job giving you Godly principles that are practical. These same principles will help you when you're STUCK. It was an honor to write the foreword for this book because I know that the content will change the lives of everyone who reads it.

Cecilia L. Lester

Wife. Mother. Follower of Jesus.

PART I

Where is my Jack?

Chapter 1

WHEN TIRES GO FLAT

In need of a Spare

One of the most nerve-racking traveling experiences outside of a minor car accident is discovering that a tire has gone flat. Virtually everyone has experienced a flat tire, either through personal experience or while riding with a friend or family member. It is never a fun occurrence, and it typically happens unexpectedly. If you have not experienced a flat tire, just keep riding or driving, it will eventually happen. Perhaps you'll have to either change a tire or watch someone else perform the task. Wouldn't you agree that flat tires seem to occur during the most inopportune times? Maybe you were preparing for a night out on the town, going to visit a friend, en route to school or work, or even on the way out of town for a much needed vacation. Next, a loud burst or a strange thumping sound startles you. "What in the world was that?" you ask yourself.

Seconds later you are answered by a shaking car and a wobbly steering wheel. If you are traveling outside of your neighborhood at night or in an unfamiliar area, the fear of being stuck on the side of a dark road or expressway may enter your mind immediately. Instantaneously, your mental processes go into

2

interrogation mode. Thousands of variables rush through your mind.

Your fragmented thoughts might go something like this: "Side of the road ... by myself ... what if I do not have a spare? ... I'm stuck ... where is the jack? ... who will help me? ... nobody is home ... cell phone battery is dying ... What if I have to get a

> Isn't it funny how the slightest adversity causes us to question our journey?

tow truck?" You are in shock. After all, you were headed somewhere, weren't you? You were clear of your destination, but the unexpected happened. "What if I miss my appointment?" you say to yourself—believing you will. Isn't it funny how the slightest adversity causes us to question our journey, ourselves, or even our decision to go in the first place?

Finally, your shaking car makes it to the side of the road, and another unexpected event occurs. Your cell phone battery unexpectedly dies, and you cannot find the tire jack.

"It was there the last time I looked; now it is missing. Where could it be?" you mutter under your breath.

Knowing there is a strong chance you will not arrive at your destination as planned, your disposition changes. No longer are you in the same mood you displayed before leaving the house. You take a deep sigh, "Inhale...exhale..." Your life becomes the movie in which you are the pessimistic critic. Doesn't it seem that when we experience unexpected events, it provokes us to count all the negatives and lose all strength?

"These types of things always happen to me ... I can't believe my cell phone is dead ... I'm always by myself ... I should have never tried to go anywhere ... It seems like bad things happen to me a lot ... My life is hard ... I should just give up!" Slowly, the flat tire takes on a life and existence of its own. It now has a metamorphosis! The flat tire is no longer an inanimate object on the car; instead it becomes part of your mental process. For a little while, it literally takes over!

Everything inside you goes flat. Your thoughts go flat. Your intrinsic motivation, drive, and morale go flat. Your attitude goes flat. Your strength goes flat. Your desire dwindles, and your hope flattens right along with the awkwardly deflated enemy. There is a familiar Proverb that says, *"If you faint in the day of adversity, your strength is small."*[1] Often times our strength deflates not because we are void of physical strength or goodness, but because we choose not to find strength in God during flat moments.· We allow the enemy to start a war in our minds and forget to invite God to aid us in the enemy's attack. Without knowing it, ruminating on what went wrong for an extended period of time leads to a melt down or even causes depression to happen.

---

[1] Proverbs 24:10, New King James Version.
· It is important to believe that God is all you need when you feel alone or stuck. People make the mistake of using externals to provide strength when they feel stuck internally. Some people create noise so they do not have to deal with the internal noise that is going on inside them.

More than flat tires

We all know what flat tires equate to – being stuck! Finding ourselves in such a fix can produce many negative emotions. If we are not careful, we might easily view life through a negative pervasive lens. It is just as easy as what Bob Phillips writes in his book, *Controlling Your Emotions Before They Control You*:

> It is difficult, if not impossible, to read newspapers and magazines that do not regale us with murder, betrayal and disaster. Television is filled with soap operas and talk shows that deal with every possible form of wickedness and sexual deviation. Not only have the national and international problems increased, but individual difficulties are also on the rise. Billions of dollars are spent annually in dealing with mental health. Tons of barbiturates are consumed daily by people trying to cope with life. Mental hospitals and psychiatric clinics are crowded with hurting people. Suicide is still one of the major causes of death. Nervous breakdowns, stress disorders, and emotional exhaustion are common in many families.[2]

Many people's lives have caught flats; depression and dejection have taken over their minds. In fact, being stuck is not

---

[2] Bob Phillips. *Controlling Your Emotions before They Control You*. (Eugene, Oregon: Harvest House Publishers, 1995), 7.

always about something physical. Being stuck could very well be an internal state. In *Telling Yourself the Truth*, William Backus and Marie Chapian write, "Our thoughts determine our behavior. When we speak of behavior, we mean not only our actions but also our emotions."[3]

King Solomon had it right in the book of Proverbs: *"For as he thinks in his heart so is he."*[4]

Solomon, one of the wisest kings on earth, recognized the power of a thought and belief system. He knew that our beliefs have the power to work for us or to become our worst enemies. He knew that the mind was a battlefield and in constant need of God's truth. Additionally, he understood the authority God divinely wired within our cognitive ability. Given modern day scenarios, he would have been able to readily conceptualize the fact that a single thought can spark an idea that could take mankind to space, another thought could revolutionize the world with the creation of the Internet, yet another thought could discover cures and medical vaccines to save lives, and one thought could lead an entire nation.

However, just as thoughts can work in our favor, they also can work against productivity or positive action. The heinous crime committed on September 11, 2001 was first a single thought in a deranged and evil mind. This single thought was enlarged, augmented, and cultivated until it played out before our very eyes on television, and for those living in New York City, in living

---

[3] William Backus and Marie Chapian. *Telling Yourself the Truth*. (Bloomington, Minnesota: Bethany House Publishers, 2000), 26.
[4] Proverbs 23:7, New King James Version.

color! Just as this act proved deadly and destructive in a physical sense, negative mental and emotional activity can also bring about a slower and perhaps less apparent death. Sooner or later, you will realize that something is not working out for your good; and in time, unless some changes are made, others will do the same.

Check your air

We literally can come to a place in life where, mentally and spiritually, we have a difficult time trying to move forward inwardly. It is easy to identify this feeling because it will feel like all your air of belief, faith, and sense of worth has leaked out.·

> People who are stuck normally speak from thoughts of rumination.

This lack of forward mobility is largely controlled by what we think—the ideas and attitudes which we embrace. Mainly, this difficult time stems from our self-talk. "Self-talk means the words we tell ourselves in our thoughts. It means the words we tell ourselves about people, experiences, life in general, God, the future, the past, the present; it is specifically, all of the words you say to yourself all of the time."[5] It's just that simple, our "self-talk" determines if we become stuck internally. If you are "stuck" internally, try going on a long journey, you will not travel far.

We should never be comfortable with thinking or making statements to ourselves that have the power to stop us in dead in

---

·This is what depression does. It makes a person feel like life is empty and it will never be full again.

[5] Backus and Chapian, 28.

our tracks. We must stop believing lies and negative self-talk, and become familiar with God's truth. Often times, how God views us is totally different from how we view ourselves. God views us through the lens of love, while negative "self-talk" can cause us to view ourselves through the lens of guilt, shame, unworthiness, and lowliness if we are not careful. Negative "self-talk" causes us to reject ourselves.

"If we do not know the truth, we will come into bondage. One of Satan's greatest assets is an unrenewed mind that is full of worldly wisdom. When we resort to thinking with reason and logic, devoid of the wisdom and knowledge of God, we will fail every time and wind up doing the will of the enemy."[6]

A psalm written by David gives us parameters on how we should speak. He writes, *"Let the words of my mouth and the meditation of my heart be acceptable in Your sight, O LORD, my strength and my redeemer."*[7] This psalm admonishes us not to speak or think anything unacceptable to the ears of God. Therefore, we should alleviate any words or thoughts that would displease God, or not be beneficial to ourselves. If we choose not to stop these negative words, they will continue to cause our mental, spiritual, and physical tires to deflate.

Where did you stop?

You can always tell how stuck people are based on their thoughts, emotions, behaviors, and statements. People who are

---

[6] Burton Stokes and Lynn Lucas. *No Longer A Victim*. (Shippensburg, PA: Destiny Image Publishers, 1988), 15.
[7] Psalm 19:14, New King James Version.

stuck normally speak from thoughts of rumination. "Rumination is dwelling on negative thoughts for long periods of time."[8] For instance, maybe you started school but became discouraged midway and got stuck. You finished half of your required classes, but lost your momentum, and then stopped because you constantly told yourself you couldn't finish. Now years have gone by and you are thinking about school again, and since it has been so long, you don't know if you can complete the work because you question yourself and your ability. Self-doubt has laid the foundation for a small and restrictive prison and you seem hopelessly stuck. In other words, you have embraced a totally false thought that, like a vengeful spider, has spun a dysfunctional emotional web. Therefore, you have responded not to your true worth, value, and potential, but to the emotional feeling, not the actual thought itself. "If Satan can turn a truth into a lie, and make us believe that it is truth, we will cleave to it, act upon it and it will bring forth death."[9] This death plays out in emptiness and a feeling of unworthiness in life – Simply put, depression and dejection.

Flat thoughts

Cognitive Behavioral Therapy is an area in the counseling field used to help individuals deal with dysfunctional emotions produced by faulty thinking or perception. A young psychiatrist named Aaron Beck developed the Cognitive Behavioral Theoretical approach during the 60's. "Beck developed the

---

[8] Stephen S. Ilardi. *The Depression Cure: The 6-Step Program to Beat Depression Without Drugs.* (Cambridge, MA: Da Capo Press, 2009), 11.
[9] Stokes and Lucas, Ibid.

approach to challenge Sigmund Freud's orthodoxy of physiotherapy."[10] It was Beck's idea that depression was caused by an ocean of negative thoughts occurring over and over in the brain. He challenged Freud's thought because Freud held that a person had to dig deep into his or her childhood to deal with depression, which normally called for a client to do three to four days of work per week. Beck's approach concluded that thoughts matter, and if thoughts are controlled depression would lift. "To a large degree, cognitive behavior therapy is based on the assumption that a reorganization of one's self-statements will result in a corresponding reorganization of one's behavior."[11] In other words, it suggests that a large part of our reality stems from our response to our thoughts.

Our thoughts become the potter that shapes our behavior, inner feelings, and emotions. We must identify false thoughts that come up because they have the power to cause us to look through lenses that are totally false. In fact, negative thoughts equate to contaminated lenses or worldviews. Never assume that where you are or what you have gone through is the "be all and end all." You can be in one place today, and if you believe you'll be there always, that false thought could cause you to create a permanent residence in a place you were only passing through. I love David's words in the twenty-third psalm. He observes around verse four

---

[10] Ilardi, 53.

[11] Gerald Corey. *Theory and Practice of Counseling and Psychotherapy,* Eighth Edition. (Belmont, CA: Thomas Brooks/Cole, 2009), 275.

that we "walk through the valley of the shadow of death."[12] He held an idea that God would bring him out on the other side of the valley (not making the valley a permanent residence). It is when we think the valley is forever that we become stuck. That's why Paul the Apostle admonishes, *"Finally, brethren, whatever things are true, whatever things are noble, whatever things are just, whatever things are pure, whatever things are lovely, whatever things are of good report, if there is any virtue and if there is anything praiseworthy—meditate on things."*[13] His words are not empty. Why? Paul wrote this letter from a prison. He had every right to possess negative thought processes, but he chose to focus on God and his purpose instead.

Maybe you had a bad relationship or you experienced geographical relocation, divorce, the death of a loved one, or physical or mental abuse. It has been months or even years since you have given another relationship a try. You protect yourself by not getting involved with anyone, or you may do what Henri Nouwen suggested in his book, *With Open Hands,* hide behind distractions and run from pain. In fact, you have become a master of self-induced isolation. You have erected an iron barricade around your heart and have hidden the key—even from yourself. You secretly fear that every man or woman will eventually disappoint you. These are the thoughts that have become your life. Your deepest desire is to give it one more shot, but you have great

---

[12] Psalm 23:4, New King James Version.
[13] Philippians 4:8, New King James Version.

difficulty moving beyond your hurt from the past. You feel stuck and alone. This feeling may be identified as fear. "Fear induces us to erect high walls of protection around ourselves. Therefore, healthy interaction is impossible and we do not learn how to receive or give love."[14]

Maybe you started out in pursuit of a marvelous dream. After many rejections, you placed your unique talent and gifts on hold, tossed your dreams in the trash, or politely placed them on a shelf where nobody could see them. The rejection you experienced became the lens in which you viewed the world. The pain of not being accepted may have been unbearable. Through this process, you feel you have solved your problem because seemingly you do not have to deal with things moving slower than anticipated, or not moving at all. This too, is a lie, because when we deny ourselves the right to freely express our gifts and talents, we become frustrated and deny a part of ourselves. Therefore, a false sense of failure becomes internalized based on our faulty thought patterns. Responding to negative thoughts, dysfunctional emotions, and a faulty disbelief system can become the nail that pokes a hole in your dream and your self-esteem. These nails, if given power by your thoughts and rumination, can flatten your dreams and your interior life altogether. There is a Proverb that says, *"Hope deferred makes the heart sick, but when the desire comes it is the tree of life."*[15] Just because your heart has been sick does not mean

---

[14] Stokes and Lucas, 193.
[15] Proverbs 13:12, New King James Version.

that life is not forthcoming. It's been years since you have tried to sing, dance, play an instrument, act, or utilize your talent. In essence, you are stuck.

Thoughts about the rejection you have experienced have deposited false emotions of unworthiness or shame and have stopped you dead in your tracks. However, now you understand that staying in this place is not worth it. Just as Roadside Service or a friendly passerby may provide assistance in getting back on the road after a flat tire, God's power provides the much needed "spare" and restoration to continue the journey. He can even use your rejection (flat tire) as a springboard for a greater impact. You might be late for your original destination but just in time for an even more rewarding appointment. The scriptures remind us that God uses all things for our good (Romans 8:28). That includes the good, bad, and indifferent. Maybe you are that person who started attending church and vowed to work on your relationship with Christ, and before you could do so, you were hurt and turned off by counterfeit, disappointing, and puzzling behavior displayed by some so-called fellow Christians. Now, you have even questioned God and have become spiritually stuck. You've put your relationship with God on hold because you thought His believers should have represented Him in a good way. You may have wondered if indeed God condoned the way these people behaved, and instead of going directly to Him, you may have assumed that this is the way the Kingdom operates. Those thoughts have transformed into bitterness not only toward people, but toward God too. Instead of reading the Bible and attending church regularly, your desire to be involved in church has decreased and become as flat as the most air-deprived tire that you may have ever encountered. However, our perception of God must never be based upon the behavior of people. Why? Because human behavior is fickle and inconsistent. Jesus is the only one that never changes (Hebrews 13:8). Our foundation must come only from the sole mediator, Christ Himself. The scripture teaches, *"For there is one God and one Mediator between God and men, the Man Christ Jesus.*"[16] We must also remember that we are all imperfect people seeking a perfect, Holy, and sovereign God. Whenever we do not understand something, or have become frustrated with others—we must give it all to God, and ask Him to lead the way.

Or maybe you have always been a skeptic or unbeliever. Christianity turned you off before you even gave it a try, but you have always wondered about the Creator of heaven and earth (Psalm 121:2). You have always been inquisitive but allowed people's misrepresentation of God to turn you away. Therefore, your quest for truth and God has become stuck.

Perhaps you could be the Christian who started off really well; you attended church and have confessed being a Christian for a number of years. Your ability to quote the Bible without looking up a verse was impressive. You prayed often and even served in a ministry setting, but you committed a sin that caused you to be treated differently or even cast out from your church.

---

[16] 1 Timothy 2:5, New King James Version.

Subsequently, you were removed from your ministry role. You too, are "stuck." Remember: God can restore you (Psalm 51:12).

In many instances, either one of these categories could have been us, similar to us, or is currently our reality. During these times, we must be assured God is an ever-present help in times of trouble and affliction (Psalm 46:1). During these times, God

> Let God give you the right fuel or spare so you'll be in a position to overcome being stuck.

does not want us trying to change our flat situation alone and with our own strength; He wants to help. God is waiting on you to pick up the phone of your heart and ask for His help. He will become the roadside service that will come along side you just in time. The scriptures are true when they say, *"Have you not known? Have you not heard? The everlasting God, the LORD, The Creator of the ends of the earth, Neither faints nor is weary. His understanding is unsearchable. He gives power to the weak, And to those who have no might He increases strength."*[17] Allow God to give you the right internal air or spare so you'll be in a position to overcome being stuck.

---

[17] Isaiah 40:28-29, New King James Version.

Getting Past Stuck
CHECK UP

Points to ponder

1. Unexpected events happen all the time, but we should never allow them to stop us from moving forward in life.
2. We must prepare for the unexpected by strengthening our faith in God.
3. Our thoughts guide the direction in which our life moves.
4. God gives us spares when life causes flats.
5. It is never too late to start again.
6. Never change your plans, just change your route.
7. God is able to refuel you inwardly.

Focus Scripture

"Brethren, I do not count myself to have apprehended; but one thing I do, forgetting those things which are behind and reaching forward to those things which are ahead."

-Philippians 3:13

Chapter 2

HELP! I'M STUCK!

Taking responsibility

It is crucial to take responsibility for your thoughts and behaviors after you become aware of your faulty thoughts. One of the main goals in the Cognitive Behavioral approach is to identify what is true and what is a pattern of negative thoughts. "Beck thought that if people would write down negative thoughts people would be able to examine their emotions and behaviors through a lens of reason."[1] If you do not know what has caused some of your thought processes, or what triggers the negative emotions that make you want to stop altogether, I challenge you to explore your thoughts and emotions to pinpoint what is going on inside. You'll be surprised by the number of people who do not understand why they are behaving or thinking the way they do. Most haven't explored their thoughts and emotional triggers. It is true that "before we can get to where we're going, we need to know where we are. When it comes to understanding our own emotions, this is where most of us are lost."[2] Most people like to play "hide and

---

[1] Ilardi, 55.
[2] Douglas Stone, Bruce Patton and Sheila Heen. *Difficult Conversations: How to Discuss What Really Matters*. (New York, NY: Penguin Group, 1999), 91.

seek," looking all around them instead of taking an inward inventory of why they feel as they do; and why they are where they are in life. I absolutely love what Wayne Cordeiro wrote in his book, *Leading on Empty*: "Our lives are like notebooks. Some are lived with empty pages—nothing is written down. Others are filled with experiences, but once recorded, they are never visited again. The best lives are like notebooks whose writings are read and reflected upon over and over again. Lessons are extracted and futures are reassessed."[3] There is nothing wrong with looking into the mirror of your soul and asking God to reveal to you what does not have to be, what you can add, or how you can process what has happened. There is a blessing in becoming aware of what brought you to this point. We can discover what has stalled our progress. It has been said many times that nobody can stop us like ourselves.

> We must get past looking around and pointing the finger and start looking inside.

We must get past looking around and pointing the finger at everything and everyone for where we are in life, and start looking inside. Pointing the finger is not investigating: it's blaming and it is the easy thing to do. Do not be fooled. Blaming is one sure way to lock yourself in a prison where you are both the guard and prisoner. In fact, "Most people who don't feel content with their

---

[3] Wayne Cordeiro, *Leading on Empty* (Grand Rapids, MI: Bethany House Publishers, 2009), 97.

lives don't know the reason why. Often times they suspect that circumstances or people are to blame. They desire to change but they don't do anything different so they can change. They merely hope things will turn out right—and become frustrated when they don't."[4]

We cannot solve our problems by relying upon old habits, decisions, feelings, and thoughts. Trying to solve an existing problem with an "old" (wrong) answer is like having a car and trying to crank it up with a door key; you'll never leave the driveway. However, you must be willing to look for the right key and believe that God will help you find it. Sometimes just taking responsibility for the inward search is enough.

In his book, "Reaching Out," Henri Nouwen regards this as turning loneliness into solitude. He suggests that a person must embrace their inward pain in order to discover what must be conquered. I love David's thought in Psalm 139:23-24, *"Search me, O God, and know my heart; Try me, and know my anxieties; And see if there is any wicked way in me, and lead me in the way everlasting."*[5] The truth is that no one can determine our outcome like God, who is in control of everything. Of course we play an intricate role in the outcome based upon our decisions and responsibilities, but we must become open and transparent and give God something to work with.

---

[4] John C. Maxwell. *Thinking for a Change*. (New York, NY: Warner Books, 2003), 27.
[5] Psalm 139:23-24, New King James Version.

Being stuck hurts

Acknowledging pain is half the battle. Once you are able to locate a pain's origin (diagnosis), you can know how you must care for the pain (prognosis). Even medical doctors cannot operate until they identify what areas need attention.

Just as being ill, having a serious injury, or being involved in a severe accident causes physical pain; one of the most painful feelings in the world is that of being stuck internally. Being tortured by the thought of being unable to move beyond present hardships becomes the thorn in your side that causes you to give up on life. It is discouraging to spin your tires in the wet mud of stagnation. It is even more disheartening to feel that every effort, prayer or goal always eludes you. Although this feeling is painful, this does not mean that God will not cause an internal emotional healing to occur in your life with the right work (processing and working through your ideas with application). God always has the last say when it seems like you're infected with the feeling that you will be stuck forever. God has the last say in our outcome (prognosis), period. Additionally, you need not be perfect for God to help you. You only have to believe in His Son and His power (Romans 10:9-12).

The BIG question(s)

Let's slow down for a moment. I have a couple of very important questions to ask you. They may be some of the most challenging questions you will ever have to face. They are questions that no one in your personal life can answer. Your spouse, teacher, best friend or pastor: they cannot answer these questions for you.

These questions are personal and have the capability to provoke you to stare into the mirror of your soul. Similar to the navigational systems upon which we have grown increasingly dependent, the answers can help to inform you as to the global positioning of where you are in life so that you will have a better idea of turns and adjustments needed to reach your goals. In other words, you must first acknowledge that you need directions before you can find out where you are. The worst mistake you can make is thinking you are not lost when you are. This causes people to be stuck for years. The Bible is true when it suggests, *"God will direct our paths."*[6] However, we must first trust God to direct what we cannot control ourselves. We must release control of our vehicle and allow Him to take the wheel.

The BIG questions are simple. Are you stuck? And if so, where did it happen? Before you answer these questions, if you have never felt this way, let's summon the local physician because there is a slight chance your pulse has been altered. In fact, there will be times where life, as you know it, will seem like it is moving forward out of routine. It may seem that you are on autopilot, yet inwardly you feel that every possible hope, dream and goal has been frozen in time. Let's look at the simple STUCK test.

STUCK TEST

You'll know you're stuck if:

---

[6] Proverbs 3:5-6, New King James Version.

S- You cannot **See** anything better forthcoming.· The lens through which we view life plays an important role in how our life plays out. In fact, it is vision that aids us in pursuing the vision God has for our lives. However, *"where there is no vision, people perish."*[7] People who have become stuck normally profess that they do not know where they are or where they are going. The loss of sight means a loss of direction.

T- You **Talk** about negatives more than you talk about possibilities. Rumination is one of the main causes of negative speech. It focuses us on pessimistic ideas for long periods of time. The words of our mouths create springboards that push us forward or mud that keep us stuck. If you have spoken more about the problem than about solutions, you could be stuck. People who become very negative and pervasive in their thinking usually are unable to see any way out.

U- You are **Unable to receive help** because of pride or feelings of worthlessness.· We can make wrong assumptions about our current positions; therefore it is always smart to have those around who can help. Not asking for help when you need it is hard at times, but pays great rewards. It is often times easier to take it on by yourself than to let people in. However, it is important to know that you

---

· One sign of depression is hopelessness, and a lost of interest in all normal activities for an extended period of time. We must be cognizant that where we are physically and emotionally is not permanent. Most people cannot see better for themselves because they identify who they are with where they are.
[7] Proverbs 29:18, King James Version.
· Being stuck also causes people to isolate themselves from others, or feel they are unworthy to receive help.

cannot handle everything alone. If you refuse to let those around you aid in changing your internal flat, you may be stuck. It would be wise to discard any pride and receive the help extended.

C- You **Compromise** easily. Giving in to compromise can cause a person to make wrong decisions repeatedly. These wrong decisions can keep a person where they are for a long time. Several things could contribute to our compromises. We can be persuaded to compromise by relationships, habits, past mistakes, or our current environments. If you are not careful, each of those things could cause you to compromise God's best for your life.

K- If you **Keep** where you are internally a secret. One of the worst places to be is in a place where you are hiding how you feel. Imagine being on the side of the road in need of help, but no one could see you, and worse, you do not tell anyone you are there. Sometimes it's best to talk it out with those around you. If you are hiding a flat, then you are stuck.

When God sends a spare

In the Second Book of Kings, 7:3-9, the Prophet Jeremiah records a beautiful story of how we are to "Get Past Stuck" in the face of loss, peril, grave adversity, or when the worst occurs. It provides a case study for those times when events come out of nowhere over which we have absolutely no control.

God, through His sovereign grace, inspired Jeremiah to write a touching story that sheds illuminating light on our modern context as to how we might find a spare and change our flat tire. In other words, God allows this simple story to teach us how

24

restructuring our thoughts and perception, along with adding faith, can bring about great victory and triumph in our lives, even when we surrender. God can accomplish miraculous things in our lives when we decide to go through the pain.

2 Kings 7:3-9 records the account of four lepers sitting in dire need. They are at the end of their emotional and physical ropes. Several factors form the backdrop to these men experiencing God's deliverance and reconciliation in the most profound way.

First, during this time in history, Samaria was surrounded by the Syrian army led by a ruler named BenHadad. *"And it happened after this that BenHadad king of Syria gathered all his army, and went up and besieged Samaria."*[8] (2 Kings 6:24).

BenHadad joined forces with thirty-two other Kings in an effort to control Israel. He used an army to surround the city so no one could bring food in or take it outside of its gates. (2 Kings 20:1) Samaria during this time was the capital of Israel and under the leadership of Ahab. The four men at this point are cast out of the city for their leprosy. Individuals affected by this dread disease would be sent away until they were made clean from their affliction (Leviticus 13:3-4). Could you imagine being among God's chosen people in the midst of having enemies trying to control your existence? Their plight was even more complicated because, in addition to being a part of the attacked and besieged population, they were also ostracized because of their leprous condition. What a position in which to find oneself! Externally, at

---

[8] 2 Kings 6:24, New King James Version.

this point, your people are under attack and rendered powerless, and internally, even *they* do not want you around. I offer this as a classic illustration of being stuck! The four men are on the verge of dying and find themselves stripped of everything. I can only imagine what type of thoughts they entertained. Their thoughts were probably extremely flat at this point. All hope of making it out alive had probably long since died.

The defining question

Through all of the disgust and anguish, one of the lepers to musters up an ounce of faith to go forward; even if it meant facing pain from their enemies. It pierces his thoughts and enters his heart and mind. By asking "Why are we sitting here until we die?" he is simply asking, "What can we do to move out of the position of being stuck?" In other words, he was questioning their thought processes and failure to identify options.

Immediately, that single thought gave energy to a domino effect that brought great redemption and restoration. Let's look at the scripture, and see how the story unfolds:

"Now there were four leprous men at the entrance of the gate; and they said to one another, "Why are we sitting here until we die? If we say, 'We will enter the city,' the famine is in the city, and we shall die there. And if we sit here, we die also. Now therefore, come, let us surrender to the army of the Syrians. If they keep us alive, we shall live; and if they kill us, we shall only die." And they rose at twilight to go to the camp of the Syrians; and when they had come to the outskirts of the Syrian camp, to their surprise no

one was there. For the LORD had caused the army of the Syrians to hear the noise of chariots and the noise of horses—the noise of a great army; so they said to one another, "Look, the king of Israel has hired against us the kings of the Hittites and the kings of the Egyptians to attack us!" Therefore they arose and fled at twilight, and left the camp intact—their tents, their horses, and their donkeys—and they fled for their lives. And when these lepers came to the outskirts of the camp, they went into one tent and ate and drank, and carried from it silver and gold and clothing, and went and hid them; then they came back and entered another tent, and carried some from there also, and went and hid it. Then they said to one another, "We are not doing right. This day is a day of good news, and we remain silent. If we wait until morning light, some punishment will come upon us. Now therefore, come, let us go and tell the king's household."[9]

The leper who spoke up grew tired of being in his position. He understood that having thoughts of death would not help them overcome. He searched his thoughts and emotions and found the strength to speak up and challenge where they were. He allowed one thought to spark the faith needed to move forward. He understood they had nothing to lose. If they stayed in the position they are in nothing happens, and if they move forward, nothing may happen. However, their faith created an opportunity for them to gain a massive victory. I encourage you grab your Bible and read the entire story to find out more great things God did for

---

[9] 2 Kings 7:3-9, New King James Version.

Israel as a result of His grace toward the lepers as they were about to surrender to their enemies camp.

How you look at your situation

There are documented stories in which two people are diagnosed as terminally ill with the same disease and of similar severity and progression. It is a matter of perspective; however, some would describe this situation as being stuck in affliction and trouble.

One individual hears the diagnosis, goes home, calls his family together and plans a funeral. He begins to dispose of certain cherished items. His countenance changes immediately and his condition rapidly declines.

The other individual looks at the doctor, acknowledges that he indeed heard the gloomy assessment, and proceeds to go on a cruise already planned or perhaps starts looking for a new home or redecorates the old one. Within, a deliberate decision has been made. "As long as I live, mine will be a good life. This death sentence does not have to be!"

> Now is the *best* time to place everything in God's hands and say to yourself, "What do I have to lose?"

Not too long following, the first individual has become so ill that he cannot remain mobile. On the other hand, the second person is, in the words of the old Baptist hymn, "running on to see what the end is going to be." In fact, he gives little thought to the end. Instead, he gratefully focuses on the present day and the gift that comes with it.

Are you in a place where you are asking yourself, "Why am I staying in the same place and not moving forward?" Now is the *best* time and place to surrender to God, face the pain inside, and say to yourself, "What do I have to lose? Moving forward can only put me in a better place." It's time to discard all negative thoughts and false emotions and move forward. We must decide to "Get Past Stuck." It begins with the first step. If you've ever felt you were small, insignificant or outnumbered, God can empower your steps.

Another interesting feature of this story is that after the leprous men received this mercy filled victory, they agreed among each other that they should share the good news. This is symbolic of our sharing personal victories with others after God has allowed us to overcome. There is something special about sharing good news with others. John the Revelator penned these words in the Book of Revelation, *"And they overcame him by the blood of the Lamb and by the word of their testimony."*[10] It ignites faith in others to believe God in spite of their current problems. It not only encourages the next person, it reminds you that if God came through once, He will remain by your side every time you feel stuck. No matter how He decides to move, we should remain confident that He is able!

---

[10] Revelation 12:11, New King James Version.

Did the physical signs of leprosy disappear right away? Definitely not! Ongoing faith was required of all of them. However, they were in a different place than where they started out. They were divinely moved ahead toward restoration by facing their pain. You must start moving to get past where you are. If not, you could be stuck forever.·

Moving forward is a process. First, you become aware; this helps you to clearly identity what has you stuck. Second, you prepare yourself; gather the wisdom you'll need to move forward. You should never move until you have the proper advice. Thirdly, you implement; take ownership and implement the wisdom you have gathered. Fourthly and last, you must follow through; this is where you become consistent in keeping your promise to yourself.

Like the lepers who decided to take responsibility for where they were and face their enemies, you need not have all of your ducks lined up perfectly before you move forward to face your inner pain. In fact, the best time to move forward is when all control is admittedly out of your hands and finally in God's hands. Who's to say that you are not exactly where God would have you in this season of your life? I love a remark by Oswald Chambers: "Not even the smallest detail of life happens unless God's will is behind it."[11]

I remember reading a story by an unknown author that sheds a little light on how God will use the most uncomfortable

· Some forms of depression become hard to recover from if not treated properly.
[11] Oswald Chambers. *My Utmost for His Highest: Graduate Edition*. (Grand Rapids, Michigan: Discovery House Publishers, 1995), July 16.

places to show us He is in control and will never leave us (Hebrews 13:5). Here is the story, entitled "Shipwreck":

Shipwreck

> The only survivor of a shipwreck was washed up on a small, uninhabited island. He prayed feverishly for GOD to rescue him, and everyday he scanned the horizon for help, but none seemed forthcoming. Exhausted, he eventually managed to build a little hut out of driftwood to protect himself from the elements and to store his few possessions. One day, after scavenging for food, he arrived home to find his little hut in flames with smoke rolling up to the sky. The worst had happened! Everything was lost! He was stunned with disbelief, grief, and anger. "GOD, how could you do this to me?" he cried. Early the next day he was awakened by the sound of a ship that was approaching the island. It had come to rescue him. "How did you know I was here?" asked the weary man of his rescuers. "We saw your smoke signal," they replied.[12]

It's easy to get discouraged when things seem stuck, but God is in control and working out every situation in our lives, play-by-play. I pray that you will become sensitive to God's voice, so He may lead you into your next victory on the inside. It is He and He alone who can help each of us to get past stuck and into total fulfillment in our lives. So set your expectation high, and get ready to move past stuck. In the coming chapters, we will look at

---

[12] Unknown Author.

various principles from the lepers' story, and see how we can apply their wisdom to our specific situations.

Each following chapter will include parts of the lepers' story so we may gather insight from a biblical perspective on how we too can, "Get Past Stuck."

Getting Past Stuck
CHECK UP

Points to ponder

1. We must examine ourselves and take responsibility for where we are in life.
2. We must end all blaming.
3. Feeling stuck is a real feeling, but it does not have to be permanent.
4. Being stuck is a great opportunity to look in the mirror to evaluate, adjust, and improve ourselves.
5. God will restore you and allow you to make a comeback.
6. We must place everything in God's hands, not our own. It is our faith in Him that will help us move forward from where we are.
7. The best time to move forward is when you admit that all control is out of your hands and finally in God's hands.

Focus Scripture

"The steps of a good man are ordered by the LORD, and He delights in his way. Though he fall, he shall not utterly be cast down; for the LORD upholds him with His hand."
-Psalm 37:23-24

Chapter 3

LETTING GOD IN

---

[3] *"Now there were four leprous men at the entrance of the gate; and they said to one another, "Why are we sitting here until we die?"*

-2 Kings 7:3

Who's walking with you?

Who you go to in times of trouble determines if you will be equipped with the tools to overcome your battle, or worse, if you will be stripped of what you already possess. Going to the wrong sources for help could make your problem more complicated.· Association and alliances can make a world of difference. "The simple but true fact of life is that you become like those with whom you closely associate—for the good or bad."[1] In fact, one of the best things you might do when facing the most challenging times in life is to share with those around you who honestly care about you, and have the right counsel to help you move forward.

· There is absolutely nothing wrong with speaking to a pastor or a counselor about the issues you are facing in private. Opening up and processing information is the best way to be restored by God.

[1] John Mason. *Conquering an Enemy Called Average.* (Tulsa, Oklahoma: Insight International, 1996), 59.

34

Wrong counsel and lack of transparency keep us weak and stuck. The Bible teaches, *"Blessed is the man Who walks not in the counsel of the ungodly, Nor stands in the path of sinners, Nor sits in the seat of the scornful; But his delight is in the law of the LORD, And in His law he meditates day and night. He shall be like a tree Planted by the rivers of water, That brings forth its fruit in its season, Whose leaf also shall not wither; And whatever he does shall prosper".*[2]

Living in Western society, we have been flooded with images, brands and ideologies suggesting that when we ask for help, we are weak. "Our culture has become most sophisticated in the avoidance of pain, not only our physical pain but our emotional and mental pain as well. We not only bury our dead, but we also bury our pains as if they were not really there."[3] We sometimes feel that there must be something seriously wrong if we share our personal struggles with people who actually support us. We sometimes end up taking a "whatever" attitude, which sets us up for probable defeat. This creates an apathetic culture among our generation because it disconnects us from working out our struggles and confiding in someone who might offer good solid advice and comfort. Not everything can be solved alone. We even go all out to avoid God, healthy communities, and relationships. However, living in this isolation mode only throws more logs onto

---

[2] Psalm 1:1-3, New King James Version.
[3] Henri J. M. Nouwen. *Reaching Out: The Movements Of The Spiritual Life.* (New York, NY: Bantam Doubleday Publishing Group, 1975), 27.

an emotional, raging fire. It is dangerous to live an entire life alone as issues burn and consume your internal make-up and cause you to become more stuck (not processing what's in the closet of your mind). This could cause loneliness to feel permanent even when it doesn't have to be. I love what Dr. Gary R. Collins suggests in his book *Christian Counseling* about the loneliness we cause ourselves. "The inner feeling of loneliness comes when we perceive ourselves to be isolated from others, fail in our efforts with friends, or lack the social skills needed to relate to others. Often this sense of isolation is felt when the person is separated from God and feels that life has no meaning or purpose. Such persons need a committed and growing relationship with God, preferably within the confines of a concerned community of believers."[4]

Isolation is contrary to the nature of man and lets us know that facing life alone is not how things were originally designed for us. *"And the Lord God said, 'It is not good that man should be alone; I will make a helper comparable to him.'"*[5] (Genesis 2:18) Even the lepers had each other.

Not meant to be alone

After creating a beautiful planet in marvelous splendor filled with vegetation, animals, land, water and air, God acknowledged that something was missing in one of the creation

---

· Depression often causes a person to isolate him or herself.

[4] Gary R. Collins. *Christian Counseling: A Comprehensive Guide.* (W Publishing Group, 1988), 94.

[5] Genesis 2:18, New King James Version.

stories. He understood that man's day-to-day survival would require not only divine intervention but a human support system (a helper) as well. Let me pause here and ask: With whom can you share all that's going on in your heart without feeling they will use the information against you? Is there anyone in your life who can help you get past your current state? Have you even tried to talk to God about it? It is so difficult trying to win a battle alone; however, Christ has given us a way of escape. Clearly, the lepers discussed in the previous chapter had candid dialogue about a lot of things. Let's repeat the verse that shows this: *"And they said to one another, "Why are we sitting here until we die?"*[6]

I can only imagine they probably engaged in conversation the entire way as they walked away from the city, outcast. They may have asked questions such as: Do you miss your family as much as I do? What do you think your children are doing? Don't you miss family meal times?" The Bible says that they asked each other the hard question. "What have we done to bring us to a place where it is causing death to occur in our lives? Why did this happen to the four of us?" Now that is true examination.

The accountability they provided for each other became their spare tire. There are four benefits of keeping yourself accountable to someone close.

FOUR BENEFITS OF ACCOUNTABILITY

1. **Accountability provides a model.** Sometimes we will not know how to respond to adverse situations. However, when

---

[6] 2 Kings 7:3, New King James Version.

we are around others who do, we have a clear model as to how we are to respond.

2. **Accountability provides foresight and insight.** It is always great to glean wisdom from those around us who may have traveled the road of life a little longer than ourselves.

3. **Accountability provides protection.** If we listen carefully to the mistakes of others, we need not make the same mistakes.

4. **Accountability provides strength.** There will be times when life will knock the wind out of you and cause your strength to go flat, but if you have support, the encouraging words from those who support you will keep you inflated with hope.

At some point, I am sure the four leprous men began to challenge each other; at other times, I am reasonably sure they supported one another. But most importantly they began to dialogue, which leads to an inward sharpening and accountability. Dialoguing is the best thing we can do to start the process of moving forward. The Bible tells us that *"those around us sharpen us"*[7] and that we are *"made wise when we walk with people who are wise."*[8] By engaging in discourse, each leper found support in people who challenged their thoughts when emotions were getting the best of them. Each man became the support system each person

---

· Processing information with a counselor can be a tremendous help.

[7] Proverbs 27:17, New King James Version.

[8] Proverbs 13:20, New King James Version.

needed at this fragile time. Our biggest struggles take longer to overcome because we secretly hold things and do not share them with those closest to us. Dr. Ilardi, in his book, "The Depression Cure," asked

"What are you hiding? What thoughts are you afraid to share because you are unsure of the reception?"

You must ask yourself a hard question: *"Why am I sitting here until I die?"* What troubling set of circumstances have you chosen to accept as something you must endure? What is abnormal in your life that you are avoiding? Why are you sitting there until you die from emotional dysfunction?

This simple conversation among the lepers laid a foundation for a solid story of triumph in the Bible, an account to be retold again and again. Just ponder the profound impact that a simple, soul searching, all revealing conversation with someone who cares for you would have—especially someone who has gone through similar troubles and understands your plight.

> Our biggest struggles take longer to overcome because we do not share them with those closest to us.

Bringing it before the Throne

Maybe you are saying, "You do not know how many conversations I have had or the nights I have cried all alone because nothing has happened for me." Perhaps you can attest that you have prayed thousands of all out prayers and have seen no change. Maybe you have read books and listened to countless tapes and CDs seeking help from them. Yet nothing has changed. You even had your pastor and every strong Christian you could find pray prayers of faith and petition Heaven for change over your situation.

All of these efforts may have been helpful and temporarily comforting, but they probably have not produced lasting peace. It may be because peace is found within, by placing your faith in someone greater. We must all at some point come to a place where we do internal work to get to a place of peace. We must ask make our peace *personal*. God has to cease being something we seek in external things; we must instead start taking ownership over the peace God has freely given us through Jesus. Have you taken ownership in moving forward? Have you acknowledged that ultimately you are the one who must change your own spare tire?· Have you realized you are the one responsible for reaching out to God for yourself? You are in the best position to talk to Him directly and pray for yourself. *You* must change your own thought patterns.

The four men in the text did not ask other people to carry their leprosy for them, neither did they complain about what they did not have. If they had elected to wallow in self-pity it would have placed them in a deeper pit of despair and stuckness (or depression and dejection). They came to the point where they had to take ownership individually and talk it out. They took advantage

---

· Talking out your problems with someone (preferably a counselor) is great, but ultimately you will have to do the work for yourself.

of the privilege that God had given them and openly communicated with each other. This decision gave them power to overcome the battle in their minds. We must understand that "when opposing forces battle within the mind, whoever or whatever that controls our mind controls us."[9]

Have you communicated with God or someone trustworthy on a regular basis, or have you hidden and complained behind a flat tire? Although perhaps you have tried everything under the sun, I challenge you to pray for yourself and connect with God on a new, more intimate level. The Bible shares this amazing insight on prayer: *"Now this is the confidence that we have in Him, that if we ask anything according to His will, He hears us. And if we know that He hears us, whatever we ask, we know that we have the petitions that we have asked of Him."*[10] Jesus even gives us an assurance of the power of prayer in Mark's gospel. *"Therefore I say to you, whatever things you ask when you pray, believe that you receive them, and you will have them."*[11] Bill Hybels rightly penned in his book, *Too Busy Not To Pray:* "People are drawn to prayer because they know that God's power flows primarily to people who pray. The Scriptures are overflowing with passages teaching that our almighty, omnipotent God is ready, willing and able to answer the prayers of his followers. The miracles of Israel's

---

[9] Noel Jones and Georgianna Land. *The Battle for the Mind: How You Can Think the Thoughts of God.* (Shippensburg, PA: Destiny Image Publishers, 2006), 36.
[10] 1 John 5:14-15, New King James Version.
[11] Mark 11:24, New King James Version.

exodus from Egypt and journey to the Promised Land were all answers to prayer. So were Jesus' Miracles of stilling the storms, providing food, healing the sick and raising the dead."[12]

Prayer actually works and does so in the most profound way. What do you have to lose? I have never heard of anyone throwing up or catching a disease after praying. Nor have I heard someone say they did not feel better after prayer. Does prayer immediately solve all of your problems? *No.* However, it places you in a position for God to change you inwardly or to change the situation itself. Here is a simple prayer I have included; let's pause and communicate with God because He knows all, and knows how to get you past stuck. The Bible declares, *"The counsel of the LORD stands forever, the plans of His heart to all generations."*[13]

Personal Prayer

Dear Lord,

There is so much I have to say to You right now. Please hear my heart's cry. With my own logic, I have tried to figure my life out, and it has gotten me nowhere. I've been hurt in the past, my present, and I have hurt others with my hurt and poor decisions. Inwardly, I feel stuck. I have allowed my dysfunctional thinking, negative emotions, circumstances, blame, and negative influences to flood my mind to the point where I've wanted to give up on life, myself, and sometimes You. I do not know what to do anymore or what direction to take. I know You have a plan for my life, and I

---

[12] Bill Hybels. *Too Busy Not To Pray: Slowing Down to be with God.* (Downers Grove, IL: InterVarsity Press, 1998), 12.
[13] Psalm 33:11, New King James Version.

would love to be a part of what you have planned. I cannot live this life in my strength alone—I need YOUR STRENGTH, not my own. I know You say that You give power and strength to the weak. I need Your strength and power. I need Your Holy Spirit to come in and give me comfort and peace. Allow Your strength and peace to come into my heart and mind. Lord, give me the strength to pick up from where I am and start afresh. Father, I believe You can get me past stuck and allow me to start now. Give me the strength to work for the restoration that I know You want to give me. Give me assurance that You will never leave me nor forsake me. Help me to no longer worry about things I cannot control. Let me give You the wheel to my vehicle of life to direct and lead me. I am handing all of my flats tires over to You, and I believe You will provide me with spares that are better. Lord, if I haven't been able to articulate everything that weighs heavy on my heart, please hear my inner cry and fill the deflation that's happening within. Pump me up with joy in this moment. I want to move forward and take my relationship with You and my life seriously. Amen!

Making it personal

I'm reminded of a time I was invited to speak for a youth and young adult retreat in Knoxville, Tennessee. A local church in Marietta, Georgia decided to round up their youth, young adult groups and chaperones to take them on a retreat including visits to water parks, lots of fun, games, food, fellowship, and God. What a time it was going to be for them.

I was really humbled when they asked me to travel with them to do a three-hour workshop, dealing with identity, loneliness, and being in a covenant relationship with God. However, the morning when I arrived to speak, they were involved in a praise and worship service before it was my time to speak. There was only one thing wrong with this activity. The youth, adults and chaperones in the room were singing really softly and nonchalantly. Their lack of energy and commitment sent out a saddening message. Their body language and lack of enthusiasm seemed to say, "I really wish they would hurry up and end this stuff." They were operating out of requirement, instruction, and routine. They had absolutely no ownership of what they were singing. It was in no way personal or edifying. The director himself had to get up a couple of times and remind participants that we were worshipping God. However, his reminders and encouragement to give their best to God fell on seemingly deaf ears. The songs were still really stale, and people were acting like God was a commodity that you could purchase from the local discount store as needed and subsequently dispose of when they were pleased or had enough. Standing in the back of the room, I felt a strong authority of the Holy Spirit to go up and stop everything and start speaking. That's exactly what I did. I interrupted everything and went right into my message. It grieved me to watch the gift of praise taken for granted. It became my duty to change the mindset of a group that fell short of honoring His significance in our lives.

For an entire week, I had prepared for this message. I sought God for direction as to what He wanted me to say. Earlier that week, God filled me with passion about His people communicating with Him more. The name of the message was "Prayer Resurrection." I did not know the very message that I received from God addressed matters with which participants in that conference room were struggling. One of their major problems was they lacked basic communication with God.

The very first thing Satan attacked in the Garden of Eden was not Adam and Eve's physical body. Rather, he tampered with their communication with their Creator and with each other. Let's revisit the story in Genesis 3:1-10:

Now the serpent was more cunning than any beast of the field which the LORD God had made. And he said to the woman, "Has God indeed said, 'You shall not eat of every tree of the garden?'" And the woman said to the serpent, "We may eat the fruit of the trees of the garden; but of the fruit of the tree which is in the midst of the garden, God has said, 'You shall not eat it, nor shall you touch it, lest you die.'" Then the serpent said to the woman, "You will not surely die. For God knows that in the day you eat of it your eyes will be opened, and you will be like God, knowing good and evil." So when the woman saw that the tree was good for food, that it was pleasant to the eyes, and a tree desirable to make one wise, she took of its fruit and ate. She also gave to her husband with her, and he ate. Then the eyes of both of them were opened, and they knew that they were naked; and they sewed fig leaves together and made themselves coverings. And they heard the sound of the LORD God walking in the garden in the cool of the day, and Adam and his wife hid themselves from the presence of the LORD God among the trees of the garden. Then the LORD God called to Adam and said to him, "Where are you?" So he said, "I heard Your voice in the garden, and I was afraid because I was naked; and I hid myself." And He said, "Who told you that you were naked? Have you eaten from the tree of which I commanded you that you should not eat?"[14]

Satan knew that if he could destroy simple and basic communication with God, he could separate them from God and His perfect will. Many people are stuck not because they have no one to talk to, but because they have allowed circumstances to wedge a gap between themselves and God. How does the enemy accomplish this? Simple! All relationships are built upon communication, and whenever communication is severed with God, we leave ourselves to receive instruction from secondary sources instead of the Primary Source. Of course God will use people to advise and counsel us, but we must follow up with our own search for God. He has all the answers. Once Adam and Eve ate of the fruit, they stopped communication with God, and so they covered up themselves and hid the evidence of their disobedience.

This still goes on today. Instead of bringing their problems to God, many people use whatever is closest to cover up the problem, or receive false information from people who are not

---

[14] Genesis 3:1-10, New King James Version.

46

qualified to give them advice. Adam and Eve chose to use fig leaves. Likewise, we find all kinds of ways and things to use to hide from God. As we approach our Heavenly Father, we must learn how to make our prayers, relationship with God, and our communication personal and transparent. God and God alone will cause our situations to turn around so we can get past stuck. Our prayers, seeking his face, and desire for your situation to change must be something we want for ourselves, and not what others want for us.

I challenge you to commune with God and open up the lines of communication that the enemy has destroyed or diminished. For greater deliverance, intimate communication must exist between you and God and even between you and your own inner spirit. If you do not know what to say when you pray, revisit the prayer from earlier, or the model prayer Jesus lays out for us in Matthew 6:5-13. Both will help you formulate words until you are flowing from your heart. God requires only that we communicate with Him directly from our hearts. God is waiting on you to take that first step. He will draw near to you (James 4:8). After acknowledging that you are indeed stuck, you must ask yourself the same question that the four leprous men asked themselves. *Then you must make the strategic decision to move forward by opening your mouth! Opening your heart and mouth will start the process of healing.*

· It is important to seek counsel from licensed, certified, qualified professionals.

Getting Past Stuck
CHECK UP

Points to ponder

1. Choosing the right person(s) to talk to in times of trouble can equip us with the right healing tools/skills.

2. We must seek counsel from competent people who have our best interest at heart.

3. We must become transparent and ask ourselves the hard questions before we can move forward.

4. Never be scared to embrace accountability.

5. God longs to communicate with us through prayer. Prayer is the air that pumps up your flat tire.

6. We must take ownership of our relationship with God. We must make it personal.

7. We must remove those things that keep us from communicating with God. We must open our mouths and hearts.

Focus Scripture

"Cast your burden on the LORD, and He shall sustain you; He shall never permit the righteous to be moved."

-Psalm 55:22

PART II

Putting on my new tire!

Chapter 4

A PERSONAL FLAT

---

[4] *"... Now therefore, come, let us surrender to the army of the Syrians..."*

-2 Kings 7:4

What's your giant?

Life brings along with it many certainties. One certainty is that at one time or another, we unfortunately will all have to face some type of giant. No one is immune. Every great leader or common person has had to face some hardship or trial. For some, the giant is functioning as a single parent, head-of-household with one income and children to clothe and feed. Others have had to fight the giant of disease or other challenges that have tried to destroy their physical bodies. Some have sadly lost the battle. Some people may have had to face the brutal giants of rape, domestic violence, abuse or molestation at a young age or even in their adulthood. Some may have had to fight the giant of having a parent or sibling in which the relationship is strained.

All of these giants may have been temporarily crippling, causing one to become stuck. These four leprous men knew this all too well. They were in the middle of nowhere, in between their enemies and their homeland, battling leprosy and isolation. There

50

was even a famine in the land! Isolation, famine, and separation had become the giant that stood before them. It seemed as if every single card was stacked against them during a time they needed total support and inclusion into God's family. I wonder if these men had a clue a week earlier that they would be in their position a week later; being put out to face the giant of isolation, famine, and their enemies.

The truth is that none of us knows when we will face giants. Some of us will face some today, tomorrow, next week, a month or months from now, or even a year from now. We have no idea, but we can prepare ourselves for unexpected circumstances. Individuals often allow the temporary obstacles that they see to stop them in their tracks. I love this scripture, which explains that what we presently see is in fact temporal. *"For our light affliction, which is but for a moment, is working for us a far more exceeding and eternal weight of glory, while we do not look at the things which are seen, but at the things which are not seen. For the things which are seen are temporary, but the things which are not seen are eternal."*[1] It has been said on many occasions, "The only thing in this world that is constant is change." Who is to say you will always face what you are facing? However, you must get past what you are facing in your mind and heart before you are able to do so in reality. While giants exist, many people in the Biblical narratives overcame giants because they had great faith in a more powerful entity—God Himself! These are a few such examples:

---

[1] 2 Corinthians 4:17-18, New King James Version.

People who have overcome Giants

- **Noah** labored to build an ark made of gopher wood for one hundred years when no one believed that God had spoken to him. God used the consequent isolation to save his family and repopulate the earth. It took 100 years for the water to come. He overcame the giant of delay.

- **Abram,** born in an idol worshipping family, became a father of many nations by obeying God. God used Abram's isolation to father a family that would be his chosen people (Genesis 11 and 12). He left not knowing where God was leading him, but he still went. He overcame the giant of uncertainty.

- **Joseph** grew up in a family that hated him and his dreams. God used the pit, slavery, and a lie to promote Joseph to advise Pharaoh in a famine (Genesis 37-50). Joseph even saved his family from the famine in the land. He overcame the giant of unforgiveness.

- **Moses** led the children of Israel and faced a giant in the form of the Red Sea. God used Moses' rejection by Pharaoh too, and forced him to trust God and lead God's people out of slavery (Exodus 14). Moses was scared when God called him. He looked at his slow speech and his own imperfections. He overcame the giant of low self-esteem.

- **Joshua** overcame the giant of loss after his mentor Moses passed, gained courage, and continued to lead the children of Israel into their Promised Land. God used

Moses' death to show Joshua his true identity and God's faithfulness (Joshua 1). Joshua found his own identity in God after following his mentor for so long.

- **Jesus** was rejected by those whom He was sent to save (Psalm 118:22). That rejection led him to the cross, where He took on all the sins of the world (Luke 23:26-49). Jesus had faith that God's ultimate plan would bring redemption to all mankind by his sovereign grace (Ephesians 2:8-10). Jesus additionally knew He would become the only mediator between God and man; therefore he had complete faith. Jesus overcame the giant of rejection.

I know! I know! You are probably saying, "I know these Biblical narratives and have heard them several times." Or you could be saying, "I am not living in biblical times. I do not believe the Bible can relate to where I am currently." I share these examples with you because whether you are a believer or non-believer, only faith separates the victims from the victors. The four leprous men moved beyond where they were because they surrendered and chose to face their pain with faith, even if it meant going toward their enemies' camp. Each one of these examples had a tremendous amount of faith in God. Does it change your situation immediately? No, it doesn't, but it sparks hope and releases God to do exactly what He wills for your life.

The Biblical definition of faith is found in Hebrews 11:1: *"Now faith is the substance of things hoped for, and the evidence of things not seen.*"[2] Faith simply gives us the ability to see beyond where we are currently, and it empowers us to embrace the strength God makes available to us now. The four lepers used this faith to get past stuck. It took faith for them to say, "Let's surrender." Their surrendering meant they released control over where they were, and that gave them courage to proceed forward. Although, these men decided to surrender to their enemy's camp, God extended grace toward these men, and allowed them to gain a victory. When was the last time you surrendered and said I'm going to move forward in spite of the pain that I may have to face? Their story let's us know that God's grace is enough for us all. They refused to die where they were positioned. They were so filled with a desire to move forward that even if it did not work out as they had planned, they would have at least rejoiced that they moved and did not stay in the same place. They said, *"If we say, 'We will enter the city,' the famine* is *in the city, and we shall die there. And if we sit here, we die also. Now therefore, come, let us surrender to the army of the Syrians. If they keep us alive, we shall live; and if they kill us, we shall only die."* (2 Kings 7:4). That was bold for them to look death in the face and allow their faith and surrender to push them forward.

Are you in a place where a lack of faith has blinded you? Or were you once a very passionate Christian, but have allowed your current situation to put your spark out? I encourage you to

---

[2] Hebrews 11:1, New King James Version.

embrace faith in God wherever you are, look your dead situation in the face and say, "God's grace will allow me to defeat this giant."

Faith releases your control

Most frustrations come from our trying to control every aspect of our lives. James makes a great observation to God's governing power and authority over our lives. *"And now I have a word for you who brashly announce, "Today—at the latest, tomorrow—we're off to such and such a city for the year. We're going to start a business and make a lot of*

> When God drives our lives, the tires may go flat, but will never stay flat.

money." You don't know the first thing about tomorrow. You're nothing but a wisp of fog, catching a brief bit of sun before disappearing. Instead, make it a habit to say, "If the Master wills it and we're still alive, we'll do this or that." As it is, you are full of your grandiose selves. All such vaunting self-importance is evil. In fact, if you know the right thing to do and don't do it, that, for you, is evil."[3]

It acknowledges that God's power is more vital and potent than our own. When God drives our lives, the tires may go flat, but will never stay flat. He knows best how the vehicle of life should be driven. Paul, the Apostle, teaches God's people when he pens a letter to the Corinthian church, *"I planted, Apollos watered, but*

---

[3] James 4:13-17, The Message Bible.

God gave the increase. So then neither he who plants is anything, nor he who waters, but God who gives the increase."[4]

The church at Corinth had grown divisive and carnal. They were starting to worship Paul and his ministry partner Apollos for the great works God was using them to do. Paul quickly reminded them that though they were chosen to serve, only God was in control.

Many times we become stuck fighting the same giants because we are like the Corinthians—trying to embrace our own strength or embrace individuals without relying on God. Sometimes it is only by God's grace and strength that we are able to do anything. This is the assurance Jesus gave Paul in 2 Corinthians 12:9: *"My grace is sufficient for you, for My strength is made perfect in weakness."*[5] Jesus gives Paul confidence that when he runs out of strength; God's strength would step in.

My Personal Giant

The biggest giant I have had to face and overcome has been a mild form of clinical depression. This book serves as the spear and dagger that is killing the giant that tried to destroy my life, marriage, and ministry. Additionally, it serves as God's grace extended toward me to move forward from a place of stuckness. Depression was the nail in my mind's tire on the side of the road. Everything in my life had gone flat, and nobody knew. I was fighting the battle alone—not even my wife knew, until I decided

---

[4] 1 Corinthians 3:6-7, New King James Version.
[5] 2 Corinthians 12:9, New King James Version.

to go to counseling. It had me stuck for a year and a half! It was brutal. Sometimes I felt like I had a car accident internally and no one knew. Could you imagine going that long before you opened your mouth about the emptiness and hurt you felt on the inside? The sad part is that I brought much of the depression upon myself with worry, doubt, living in the past, ruminating, allowing what I thought others thought of me to create fear in me, and allowing myself to be disillusioned by seeking the love of God through works and achievement. Through God's grace, depression did not take me out, and I'm here to write about it, and hopefully help others who are on that road or headed that way. Trust me it is no fun. However, from this "mess" my "message" was reborn.

People of Faith Suffer

Many of you would object, "Wait, aren't you a Christian? Aren't you supposed to be happy every day of your life like nothing is wrong?" Many would question my faith if this were stated publicly in a traditional church setting; some

> We must be reminded that in this life we will have to face giants.

would claim that I was a weak Christian. We must be reminded that in this life we will have to face giants. Jesus told us often that we would endure persecution and face tribulation (John 16:33). This is why one of the fruits of the spirit is called longsuffering (Galatians 5:22-23). It instills the patience we need to go through trials. In fact, we will not be without suffering until we meet our Savior.

Sometimes church culture creates an illusion that everything has to be perfect 24/7, 365 days of the year as long as you are a Christian. This is far from the truth. It sends erroneous messages that as long as you have Jesus everything will be hunky-dory, cupcakes, and ice cream with fudge on top (ALL THE TIME). This creates weakness within church culture because people conclude that if I am suffering, maybe I do not have enough God, or maybe I am not special to God. This too is not true; we are all special to God. He loves us unconditionally but still allows us to be tested or go through periods of suffering because we live in a fallen world. The Bible says, *"God rains on the just and the unjust."*[6] We must remember that God tested Abraham with his son, Isaac, and He allowed Job's faith to be tested by the enemy himself. Job was stuck. He lost everything as a result (children, business, home, and livestock). He was even left with a wife who told him to curse God because of the suffering.

Nobody really likes to engage the thought that as Christians we will continue to suffer until we transition into eternity with God (Revelation 21:4). However, people feel that if they are suffering then it must either be the wrath of God or extreme punishment for sin. Although leprosy was the reason the four men were put out, this does not mean life couldn't have put them out without the leprosy. Some people feel that life has left them "stuck" for no reason. Every day, people are hit with unexpected flats. Sometimes you will suffer absolutely for what seems to be no reason at all.

---

[6] Matthew 5:45, New King James Version.

In his book, *You Can Be Emotionally Healed*, Dr. Morris Sheats, writes, "We suffer for three primary reasons 1) to purify the spirit, 2) to correct the soul, and 3) to join the sufferer to the body of Christ."[7] However, when suffering is looked at through the lens of obscurity, it is shunned or looked down upon. This even causes many Christians to hide secrets instead of becoming transparent and dealing with the struggles openly. I did just that. I was depressed and told no one, nor did I speak to anyone about it. There are three simple ways to become transparent:

1. Confess it to God.

2. Confess it to yourself.

3. Confess it to those whom God has placed around you to aid you, support you, and encourage you.

Even Peter writes about suffering in his first epistle: *"Beloved, do not think it strange concerning the fiery trial which is to try you, as though some strange thing happened to you; but rejoice to the extent that you partake of Christ's sufferings, that when His glory is revealed, you may also be glad with exceeding joy."*[8] Peter tells us to rejoice even in our suffering because we are a part of Christ's body.

Covering up suffering

You've probably heard it spill out of someone's mouth. You walk up to them and ask, "How are you?" and their reply is "I'm fine" or "Everything's great" as to say their life has no

---

[7] Morris Sheats. *You Can Be Emotionally Healed*. (Columbus, GA: Christian Life Publications, 1994), 96-99.

[8] 1 Peter 4:12-13, New King James Version.

problems, when sometimes this is not true at all. Perhaps you have been that person with a bright smile, while inwardly you are screaming, "HELP—SOMEBODY, ANYBODY, HELP ME!!!" That was me for *almost* two years. One of my favorite speakers, Dale Bronner, once stated in a sermon, "Secrecy only produces more weakness." Hence, the very thing that separated Adam and Eve's relationship between each other and God was secrecy and isolation. When God asked Adam where he was, Adam replied he was hiding (Genesis 3). The hiding could have very well been internal. It is my belief that this covering up (of hurts and suffering) creates illusions and produces legalistic believers who aim to overindulge in works (pursuit of accolades) to take away suffering and pain in their lives, in the world, and to please God. This was me. I kept myself busy so I did not have to face myself and my pain. I was not living a fully surrendered life. Are you distracting yourself so you don't have to deal with the pains of the past or your emotions?

Pleasing people

There was a time when my life was stuck in autopilot "Please God and people" mode. I aimed to please God and people around me. I used works to disguise what I was feeling internally. Works are simply physical efforts to replace something totally spiritual. Pleasing people became the codependency I used to make myself feel a counterfeit joy.

C.J. Mahaney defines this as legalism in his book, *Living the Cross Centered Life*. He indicated that legalism was "basing our relationship with God on our own performance."[9] We overlook that sometimes Jesus is all we need to fill the voids in our lives. We think we have to work for His love and the love of others to ease the suffering. This is not true. What God has already done on the cross is enough to save us from ourselves. C. J. Mahaney writes in the same book: "New things will always come along. Many will be useless, some will be good, a few will be better—but what's the one thing that's really best, according to God? Here's how Paul answers that question for us: 'Now I would remind you brother, of the gospel I preached to you.... For I delivered to you as of first importance what I also received: that Christ died for our sins.'"[10] Why? Because Jesus paid a price that we cannot earn through performance. It's a *free* gift. How do I know? I was that person! I had become a legalist whose only goal was to cover up my hurts, please people, and make God proud by mere works alone. During this season of my life, there were three types of people I constantly tried to please. These were even relationships that I allowed my false expectations of them push me further in a depressed state. Here are the three types of relationships:

Pleasing people

1. **Relationships with those who wanted to use me.** Trying to please this type of person is draining mentally,

---

[9] C. J. Mahaney. *Living the Cross Centered Life: Keeping the Gospel the Main Thing.* (Colorado, CO: Multnomah Books, 2006) 14-16.
[10] Mahaney, Ibid.

spiritually, and physically, and the end result is a feeling of worthlessness.

2. **Relationships with those who had nothing but negative things to say about me, and never said anything positive.** Trying to please this type of person makes you feel that the ransom God paid on the cross with Jesus is never sufficient. Therefore, you constantly try to become better to have them to accept you.

3. **Relationships with those who I hoped would notice my good, but who could have cared less.** Trying to please this type of person makes you overlook the things you should be grateful for. Trying to please such people makes you focus on outward works 24/7. It becomes a job to impress people.

Secretly, I was longing for a love that personal achievement, pleasing people, and working for God's free love could not provide for me. Only if I worked hard, had enough people accept me, and became a great success did I think God would love me. I thought that that love would take away the internal pain I was feeling within. It set me up to feel empty because I was looking for external things to fill the holes in my life. The four leprous men were placed in a position in which only God's grace could fill them, protect them, and take care of them. In essence, God was enough.

Have you tried to please people or God or hide your brokenness? The more I pursued success and love by works, the emptier I felt. This emptiness caused me to constantly look at what I did not have.

What you have left

The four leprous men moved forward because they stopped focusing on what they lacked. Sometimes we become stuck because we look too much at what we have lost, and not enough at what we have left. They were not trying to impress people, cover up their leprosy, or trust their personal strength to deliver them. They came to a point where they had to look at what God still allowed them to possess – life. I was trying to look at everything else and use external things to replace the life inside. I overlooked the treasure that had been there all the time.

What is depression, really?

There are many people who are suffering from depression, yet very few know what it truly is. In fact, it is worth knowing that millions of people each year take their life because of it. Depression is more than a common cold, or an aching stomach because you ate a bad lunch. It has some severe life-altering effects that are sometimes irreversible for long periods of time. Two of the best definitions of depression I have ever read are found in two of my favorite books. The first, *Leading on Empty*, was written by Wayne Cordeiro, a pastor who went through a bout of burnout and learned amazing lessons on his road to wellness. He wrote this book for leaders in need of restoration and practical ways to restore what depression and burnout has done to their life. The other book is, *The Depression Cure*, written by the clinical physiologist

Stephen S. Ilardi. Dr. Ilardi in his work suggested that, "it's a debilitating syndrome that deprives people of their energy, sleep, concentration, joy, confidence, memory, sex drive—and their ability to love work and even robs many people of their will to live."[11] Likewise, Cordeiro reports that there are warning signs when it comes to burnout and detection of depression. Cordeiro states, "The symptoms of depression can vary from person to person, but here are a few: sense of hopelessness, frequent tears, difficulty concentrating, decision making comes hard, irritability, insomnia, lowered activity levels, feeling alone, lack of marital attraction, eating disorders, and aches and pain."[12] I experienced all this and more. And as you can see there is nothing small about it. There are many things that cause depression, such as long periods of stress, great loss, and unresolved problems from the past or present. Of course this is not an exhaustive list of what depression is, and what it does.· I have included great books and resources in the back of this book that will help you to further discover what depression is and what it does to millions of people every year who are alive and battling it.

I changed

One of the worst parts about being depressed is that I changed. My eating habits picked up and I gained weight, information was hard to remember, it was hard for me to focus, my

---

[11] Ilardi, 26.

[12] Wayne Cordeiro, Leading on Empty (Minneapolis, Minnesota: Bethany House Publishers, 2009), 60-64.

· Depression even alters the brain.

mind constantly felt strained and conflicted, I had days where I felt extremely lonely, I battled with thoughts and ideas from my past, and so much more. Additionally, I internalized discouragement, bitterness, and anger. I had become a person who started taking out my anger on myself by coming down hard on myself. This was not normal. It seemed like all of my zeal and energy for life plummeted completely. I was extremely flat, broken, and in desperate need of help. Even my journaling as I look back on it was filled with brokenness. Here are some personal words from my journal a year and a half ago:

> *Dear Lord, today, I feel lost and empty! I believe it's because I have not been myself. The place where I am is showing me a few things: 1) I am in a place of desperation, 2) I'm seeking light in my darkness, 3) I am becoming aware of how broken I am.*

It was literally as if I felt an immense load, burden, and brokenness that I had never felt before in my life. I felt numb and had yielded to sin just to feel life again. I had become addicted to food, which I used as an anti-depressant. Something within me longed for something new and a place to be healed.

How could this be? I had gone to Bible College, was happily married, graduated with honors from a graduate degree program, authored numerous books, remained faithful in the church and ministered several times a year. I had everything anyone could want. But where did these feelings of emptiness come from? How did I ever get in this place? Seemingly, it came from nowhere, but I became aware that they had always been there. It was years of junk that I allowed to pile up and never worked through. It also came through my negative thoughts, poor self-image, and failure to verbally process all that I was dealing with inside.

Love is more than success

How did I learn I had become depressed? Simple: it was apparent that something was wrong internally. I became aware of what I was feeling inside. I identified my thoughts and emotions. Additionally, I met

> The suffering forced me to look at God more than I could have alone.

with three counselors for a combined period of a year and a half. "What could all this mean?" I asked myself repeatedly. "Am I doing the wrong things? Am I not doing enough? Am I working too much? Why is God allowing this to happen to me?" Nothing made sense as to what was causing the stress and depression because I blinded myself. I did not feel stressed or depressed most times, but I knew something was not right. Most of the time, I felt I was doing the right thing by doing so much to please God and people. I was involved to the point where it started to control my thoughts and actions. It prompted me to think negatively. I questioned God and myself because I did not know what was wrong with me, and God allowed me to become aware of my internal suffering.

Just as the four leprous men had been placed in a position of isolation to look inward, so had I. Being stuck actually saved my life. It wasn't until the pain came that I realized that I needed to heal. That's the great thing about pain—it lets you know something is wrong, and as long as you know, you can do whatever it takes to repair what's wrong. The suffering forced me to look at God more than I could have alone. It was the beginning of a long journey of discovery, healing, and learning how my thoughts ultimately led me to become depressed. I was like many Americans today—physically free and boundless, but feeling inwardly stuck and captive. During counseling sessions, I discovered that I was battling inwardly. My faulty thinking contributed to it all. My negative thoughts compounded to make me feel extremely anxious while focusing on the past (or the future), trying to resolve or deal with people who I felt wronged me, but who were nowhere to be found.

This caused me to "not cherish my now," as my counselor would say. I was consumed with impressing and blaming people, and it rewired my thoughts. I could not see the blessing God was preparing for me even during this rough time. I allowed the depression to give birth to dysfunctional emotions. Those emotions became triggers that would haunt me and cause me to behave outside of my character. My spirit and mind struggled in an invisible mud. **The more I did, the less joy I felt.** I'll never forget the life-changing questions I asked myself. How do I get past stuck? How do I deal with the issues in my life that I cover up by doing good works? How do I move forward? How do I make everything count without feeling stuck? I realized that I constantly overlooked that God loved me unconditionally, even if I did not do another thing. God's love is not contingent upon works. Once I became aware of this, I allowed God to love me just as I was.

Are you here? Have you been trying to win the love of others, and working to experience total love from a God who is already love (1 John 4:8)? I tried it, and it left me empty. It left me so empty I was left to battle a form of depression called dysthymia. An article from the February 2005 issue of the *Harvard Mental Health Letter* states the following about this type of depression:

> The Greek word dysthymia means 'bad state of mind' or 'ill humor.' As one of the two chief forms of clinical depression, it usually has fewer or less serious symptoms than major depression but lasts longer. The American Psychiatric Association defines dysthymia as depressed mood most of the time for at least two years, along with at least two of the following symptoms: poor appetite or overeating; insomnia or excessive sleep; low energy or fatigue; low self-esteem; poor concentration or indecisiveness; and hopelessness.[13]

The emptiness I experienced became so severe that it wore a hole in my relationship with my wife. I treated her badly for no reason (by shutting down and not opening up), and refused to

---

[13] Harvard Health Publications (Harvard Medical School). "Dysthymia" This article was first printed in the February 2005 issue of the Harvard Mental Health Letter.) Accessed 12 October 2010. Available at http://www.health.harvard.edu/newsweek/Dysthymia.htm

embrace the joy God blessed me with each day in the form of life. I discovered my thoughts were causing everything within me to go flat. Are you here? Have you been going through the motions? Just as the leprous men needed people to confide and look within themselves about where they were in life, so did I. And so do you.

Changing the way you think

During personal counseling sessions, I worked in seven areas to get up from where I was:

1. Thought Restructuring: This gives us the ability to identify faulty thinking. We can have thoughts that are not true, and respond to them as if they were. This is what Aaron Beck's theoretical approach is all about. We must learn to combat negative thoughts. Mainly, we should focus more on positive thoughts rather than negative ones. Looking back, I am able to see how I allowed negative thoughts that were false control my mind and behaviors. I learned to catch myself ruminating and challenge negative thoughts with positive true thoughts.

2. Healthy Perception: This gives us the ability to learn positive ways to perceive situations even when it looks and feels bad. One of my personal life coaches would tell me often that I needed to focus on the wins. It is easy to focus on all the losses around us, but it is much harder to focus on the wins we are already experiencing. Gaining a healthy perception allowed me to do this. We learn not to look at the glass half empty or half full, but to be thankful we have a glass. When we are grateful to have a glass, we are then able to fill it with whatever we desire.

3. Crisis Management: This is where we look for opportunities in crisis. For example, I was in a crisis, but profound life lessons have come out of that crisis. Without that experience I would not have penned the book you are reading. The crisis also gave me an opportunity to see all that I needed to work through internally. This awareness has made me a much healthier person because I have been able to learn skills that are showing tremendous results. Sometimes we focus so much on our immediate actions that we are blind to the good that will come out of them.

4. Exercise: I learned that exercise was life's natural anti-depressant. I learned that working out releases oxygen to the brain, and also creates healthy fatty acids that cause the brain to function properly. Working out gives me a space to think, release, and be at peace.

5. Therapy through writing: I actually started writing this book as a journal assignment about what I was facing and it ended up turning into something that I hope God will use to help others get past stuck. Writing gave me a chance to release what I was feeling. Writing is therapeutic and refreshing.

6. Prayer: This has helped me to connect with God, communicate with God, and become aware of what He desired for my life at that point. It also gave me a chance to allow God's love to become real in my life. I have learned that life should not happen apart from God. God has given me much of what I have said thus far in this book, and most importantly He has given me peace, grace, love, and the strength I needed to get past stuck.

7. Faith: Without faith I would have lacked the confidence to move forward and surrender. Each of these areas has aided me in overcoming depression.

You can't win love

It's amazing the large number of people today who look for God's love in all the wrong places. God *is* love! Have I overcome depression? I overcome it each day I focus on Jesus being enough for me, and practice the healthy skills I mentioned earlier! To get past stuck, you must work hard by restructuring your thoughts, and creating new habits. It is possible to beat depression and send it to its grave. The powers of God's love and the re-adjustment of my thoughts have helped me tremendously. No longer do I seek love by works. I have experienced the true love of God through His Holy Scriptures and through the comfort of His Holy Spirit. Sometimes the brokenness we experience happens so we will know what pieces no longer fit into our lives. Additionally, brokenness happens so that God can put us back together. There are ten blessings of brokenness that I will outline at the end of this chapter in the check-up.

Is depression a big deal? Most definitely! I believe it exists in the lives of so many people because they have never experienced real love. Many individuals are walking around depressed yet unaware of its existence. The 13th chapter of 1 Corinthians has come to be known as, "The Love Chapter." It provides a wonderful description of true love:

"Though I speak with the tongues of men and of angels, but have not love, I have become sounding brass or a clanging cymbal. And though I have the gift of prophecy, and understand all mysteries and all knowledge, and though I have all faith, so that I could remove mountains, but have not love, I am nothing. And though I bestow all my goods to feed the poor, and though I give my body to be burned, but have not love, it profits me nothing. Love suffers long and is kind; love does not envy; love does not parade itself, is not puffed up; does not behave rudely, does not seek its own, is not provoked, thinks no evil; does not rejoice in iniquity, but rejoices in the truth; bears all things, believes all things, hopes all things, endures all things. Love never fails. But whether there are prophecies, they will fail; whether there are tongues, they will cease; whether there is knowledge, it will vanish away. For we know in part and we prophesy in part. But when that which is perfect has come, then that which is in part will be done away. When I was a child, I spoke as a child, I understood as a child, I thought as a child; but when I became a man, I put away childish things. For now we see in a mirror, dimly, but then face to face. Now I know in part, but then I shall know just as I also am known.

And now abide faith, hope, love, these three; but the greatest of these is love. "[14]

The scripture above admonishes that love never fails. It suggests there is absolutely nothing we can personally do to earn love or gain more of it from our Father in heaven. He is love and He never fails. As long as we try to earn love, the more we actually push it away. How? Because, you will try to find a substitute with something that has no power to provide love. ***God's love is free!***

I hasten to add that Christianity does make available the 'Fruits of the Spirit:' love, joy, peace, longsuffering, kindness, goodness, faithfulness, gentleness, and self-control, as listed in Galatians 5:22-23. Trust me, I have experienced them all, but there are times you will not feel any evidence of these fruits. I believe the scriptures provide insight through its description of what Jesus had to endure at Gethsemane (Matthew 26: 36-44). He chose to embrace God's love, which empowered Him to overcome an agonizing pre-crucifixion experience. It is not my intent to scare you, but to offer insight so that when the time arrives to battle giants, you will not crumble under the pressure. God's love through Jesus Christ causes us to win every time.

What giant have you allowed to overpower God's promises in your life? If you ever plan on getting past "stuck," you will have to talk to someone, trust God more than your problem, embrace your faith more than your fears, lay aside external works that cover up your hurts and pains, and embrace God's love completely.

---

[14] 1 Corinthians 13:1-13, New King James Version.

> # Getting Past Stuck
> ## CHECK UP

Points to ponder

Being Broken (Ten Blessings of Brokenness):

1. **Pushes you close to God (James 4:7-8):** When we get closer to God, we find: 1) our identity, 2) direction, 3) wise counsel, and 4) how to communicate to Him through prayer.

2. **Creates hunger (Matthew 5:6):** When we hunger, we: 1) hunger for truth, 2) hunger for change, and 3) hunger for more out of life.

3. **Shows you what really matters (1 Timothy 6:6-9):** When we understand what matters, we: 1) become grateful, 2) become frugal, and 3) become a giver.

4. **Provides wisdom (Proverbs 3:13):** When we gain wisdom from brokenness, we: 1) learn from our experiences, 2) raise our standards, and 3) learn what to value.

5. **Produces humility (Jeremiah 9:23-24):** Humility happens in four areas: 1) how you hear: we become teachable, 2) how you see: we gain greater clarity and focus, 3) how you follow: we gain a heart for serving, and 4) how you lead: we understand that we must be representatives for Christ (we must lead by example).

6. **Produces Godly sorrow (2 Corinthians 7:10):** When we are broken, we: 1) learn what does not belong in our life, and 2) learn what God expects from us. We literally have a change of mind.

7. **Produces patience (James 1:2-4):** When we learn patience, we learn: 1) God's timing, not our own, 2) God's location, where we should be and why, and 3) God's instruction. We learn what to do while we wait in the place God has assigned to our lives.

8. **Provides support (Proverbs 13:20):** When we are broken, God will send, 1) counsel: people in whom we can confide, 2) models: people whom we can follow, and 3) practice: a way to display what you have learned.

9. **Provides strength (2 Corinthians 12:7-9):** We learn to, 1) depend on God's strength more, 2) trust in God's ways, and 3) build our faith.

10. **Provides purpose (Philippians 1:12):** We learn our compassions in brokenness. We learn, 1) our likes and dislikes, 2) our gifts and talents, and 3) a place to display our purpose.

Focus Scripture

"The LORD is near to those who have a broken heart, And saves such as have a contrite spirit."

-Psalm 34:18

Chapter 5

TUNING OUT THE VOICES

[4] *"....If they keep us alive, we shall live; and if they kill us, we shall only die.* [5] *And they rose at twilight to go to the camp of the Syrians..."*

-2 Kings 7:4-5

What do you hear?

Have you ever wondered why some people carry themselves with such confidence while others carry themselves with low self-esteem? Or why some people freely pursue their dreams with courage, while others take the backseat and passively waste time in absolute fear, even when God has "not given us the spirit of fear."[1] These thoughts and more have crossed my mind. I have concluded that how we behave and respond to life is more complex than our simple assumptions about unique personality types. Sure, our individual personality type plays a significant role in our identity (who we are). However, our thoughts sculpt and refine the core of our lives and how we sometimes behave. That is why the Apostle Paul encouraged us, in his letter to the Roman church, to constantly "renew our minds."[2]

---

[1] 2 Timothy 1:7, New King James Version.
[2] Romans 12:1-2, New King James Version.

76

It was Mels Carbonell, in his book, *Extreme Personality Makeover*, who stated, "This may seem confusing, but think of how most people's minds were born without major presumptions. Our personality has a certain structure with special ways of thinking, feeling, and acting. Everything we experience from birth to adolescence seems to develop our personalities into the people we become."[3]

Therefore, much of how we approach life stems from the voices we respond to that have been fashioned by our thoughts and molded by experiences of the past. Our thoughts have voices attached to them. If you do not believe me, try thinking a thought without hearing a voice; it is impossible.

You'll be surprised at the number of people who are responding to "voices of the past," the voices of people who made damaging statements during their childhood or adulthood. Sadly, they start to believe those voices, and it causes them to become completely stuck. Some people cannot get past what a parent, schoolteacher, former romantic partner, or ex-best friend said to them or about them, and in turn they start to tell themselves the same thing. Some people are still trying to work out a problem that simply needs to be let go. Instead of moving forward with their life, they are replaying an "old" flat tire (voices and negative statements) that simply cannot be patched or plugged. This alone causes major damage to the unique personality God has given

---

[3] Mels Carbonell. *Extreme Personality Makeover: How to Develop a Winning Christ-like Personality to Improve your Effectiveness*. (Blue Ridge, GA: Uniquely You Resources, 2005), 25.

them. If they are not careful, they could abort their greatness by believing things about themselves that are just not true.

Childhood voices

Many, but not all, of the voices that replay in our minds come from our childhood. "As we grow, our minds began to develop good and bad habits of thinking and processing the experiences that touched our lives."[4] Maybe you grew up in a household where you were told you were unattractive, too big, too short, too skinny, stupid, worthless, or that you would never amount to anything. This was very harmful psychological abuse. After hearing those words for years, you actually started to believe them. Now when you look in the mirror, the voice of worthlessness is tied to those thoughts that replay in your head over and over, and you feel worthless. The person who said them may not even be present anymore to make those statements. However, you have taken their place to repeat them. Those voices run through your mind on a negative auto-pilot. You have willingly told yourself countless times, "I'm worthless … no one would ever like me … I'm unattractive ... I can't do it ... It will not work … I'm a failure … I'll be just like my father or mother … or worse."

Sadly, these statements are the exact opposite of what God thinks about you. What I have explained to you was me in a nutshell. I absorbed and carried every negative statement from my past (childhood) and present (adulthood) and allowed them to consume my thought patterns. This was another element that

---

[4] Carbonell, Ibid.

created the depression in my life besides pleasing people and seeking God through legalistic, meaningless works. Responding to the voices of the past creates dysfunctional, devaluing thoughts.

Maybe you were always affirmed or given things at the snap of your fingers. You were accustomed to the proverbial silver spoon. You were told how bright you were, how you would become a great success, and how the world would bow to your feet. Now, as an adult, you do not treat people fairly. You yell at people when they do not have what you want when

> Jesus understood that what we listen to could lead us astray.

you want it. Why? Perhaps you think the entire world revolves around you. You must always be the center of attention, and it causes you to drive people away. However, being by yourself has caused you to take a deeper look at yourself. You have listened too much to the voice of entitlement and not enough to the voice of humility. We must *all* stop and ask ourselves, "What are the dominant voices shaping my thoughts?" Remember: what we listen to can cause us to become emotionally or physically stuck. The only voice we should respond to consistently is the voice of Christ. He illustrated the power of how important it is to listen to the right voice. Let's look at what Jesus said:

"Most assuredly, I say to you, he who does not enter the sheepfold by the door, but climbs up some other way, the same is a thief and a robber. But he who enters by the door is the shepherd of the sheep. To him the doorkeeper opens, and the sheep hear his voice;

and he calls his own sheep by name and leads them out. And when he brings out his own sheep, he goes before them; and the sheep follow him, for they know his voice. Yet they will by no means follow a stranger, but will flee from him, for they do not know the voice of strangers." Jesus used this illustration, but they did not understand the things which He spoke to them. Then Jesus said to them again, "Most assuredly, I say to you, I am the door of the sheep. All who ever came before Me are thieves and robbers, but the sheep did not hear them. I am the door. If anyone enters by Me, he will be saved, and will go in and out and find pasture. The thief does not come except to steal, and to kill, and to destroy. I have come that they may have life, and that they may have it more abundantly."[5]

Jesus understood that what we listen to could lead us astray. Therefore, He cautioned people to listen to the truth of His voice. He is the living Word and desires nothing but the truth to fill the voids in our lives. We must be aware that the voices we listen and respond to can influence the direction our life travels. What dysfunctional voice have you been listening to?

What voices have you stuck?

Most of us, without knowing it, respond to millions of thoughts we believe about our realities and ourselves each day; the thoughts might or might not be true. If you are angry, bitter, sad, depressed, or hopeless; if you feel worthless, betrayed, like a failure, or ungrateful, you might be listening to the wrong voices.

---

[5] John 10:1-10, New King James Version.

Whether we know it or not, the way we believe has a lot to do with the behavior we display or exhibit, or more importantly, what we choose to pursue.

Here are Ten Significant Voices that we may fight and battle against:

Ten Voices that we fight and battle against!

1. **The voice of Upbringing (Mom/Dad)** Maybe you heard negative things from your parents, and it has caused you to live your life in fear or disbelief. You subconsciously respond in your "present moment" to what they said to you years ago. Perhaps your parents said that your dreams wouldn't work out because of their personal experiences, and it crushed you. It was something you wanted to experience for yourself, but it seemed outlandish and impossible to your parents. Now when you try to do something, you do not believe you can achieve it. Or, maybe your parents praised you ridiculously and now you wrestle feeling like you will never measure up.

2. **The voice of Rejection (You are not accepted)** Maybe you experienced crushing rejection or mistreatment. Now your every decision has the echo of rejection playing in the background, which makes you fear that you will fail again, or be viewed as a worthless person. Now, you either do things to try to prove to others you are more than what they rejected or mistreated, or you seek to get even with them. John Bevere, in his book, *How to Respond When You Feel Mistreated,*

indicated "when you try so hard to prove your innocence, you quickly put yourself at the mercy of your accuser."[6]

3. **The voice of Friends (Compromise)** Maybe you are in the wrong crowd or circle of relationships, and every time you think about moving forward mentally or spiritually you hear their voices teasing you about those steps you need to take. Therefore, you embrace compromise and set aside your personal goals.

4. **The voice of Education/Intellect (What you know)** Maybe you have listened to what you have learned. You have accumulated years of education, and think you know it *all*. Therefore, you listen only to yourself and allow no one to give you a rearview or side view perspective. In fact, maybe you listen too much to your own intellect instead of having complete faith in an *all powerful* God. Reasoning and logic keep you from using your faith.

5. **The voice of public opinion/media (What others are saying)** Maybe you base your entire existence on popular opinion. You allow what everyone else thinks to determine how you feel on the inside. This is dangerous because people who live their lives centered on trends or popular opinions are never stable. You should never base who you are on what popular opinion has to say. Why? Because opinions are inconsistent. Maybe you are influenced by the voice of the media, and you base

---

[6] John Bevere. *How to Respond When You Feel Mistreated.* (Nashville, TN: Thomas Nelson Books, 2004), 28.

your decisions upon what the media presents. This could cause you to live in direct disobedience to God if you are not careful. Why? Because God may ask you to do something totally contrary to what the media is saying.

6. **The voice of Observation (What was modeled before you)** Maybe you listen to the voice of observation. You see others around you participating in dysfunctional behaviors or activities without immediate consequences, and you tell yourself it must be okay. You engage in activities that damage your life because you listen to the voice of observation. You say to yourself, "They got away with it. Maybe I can too!"

7. **The voice of Circumstance (Difficulty)** Maybe you listen too much to the voice of your circumstances. Because you are not where you desire to be, you allow your faith to be determined by what you see (that is temporary).

8. **The voice of sinful desire (Against God's will)** Maybe you are influenced mostly by your desire for sinful pleasure, and each time you sin against God, you feel weaker and weaker. This voice makes you feel that God does not love you at all because you are not perfect. Edwin Louis Cole, in his book *Maximized Manhood*, states, "Human sorrow is when we are only sorry for getting caught. God sorrow is when we are sorry for the sin, and have a desire to be rid of it."[7]

---

[7] Edwin Louis Cole. *Maximized Manhood: A Guide to Family Survival*. New Kensington, PA: Whitaker House, 1982), 29.

9.   **The voice of anger (Aggressive/ Passive)** Maybe you are
     controlled by the voice of anger. When you listen to your inner
     rage, you might destroy any and everything in sight
     (opportunities, dreams, your relationships with others, with
     God, and with yourself). This anger even causes you to hate
     yourself for it.

10. **The voice of the Enemy (The Chief Liar himself)** The enemy
     works in the framework of all these voices to make his voice
     stronger. His voice is the voice of lies and deceit. He wants you
     to believe untruths about God, yourself, and your reality. More
     than ever he wants you to be completely stuck so that you will
     forfeit the chance to move forward and become all that God
     desires you to be. He wants negative voices to become vices
     and strongholds in our lives. "Ephesians 6"[8] reminds us that the
     enemy can take form and use anything to distract us. We must
     be mindful to equip ourselves with the complete armor of God
     each and every day.

Overcoming negative voices

The leprous men have an amazing story. They illustrated
the amazing power of suggestion. Instead of thinking about all of
the people who probably said nasty, judgmental, condemning,
negative statements about them (when they were put outside the
camp), they reshaped their thoughts with their faith.

Our faith in Christ is what puts us in a place for our minds
to be renewed. *"Therefore, if anyone is in Christ, he/she is a new*

---

[8] Ephesians 6:10-20, New International Version.

creation; old things have passed away; behold, all things have become new."[9]

Recognizing negative voices in my life

My grandmother invites us over on nearly every holiday. She has been doing that since I was a child. It is easy to remember the dishes she masterfully cooked during my childhood and to this day as an adult. In fact, if you missed out on her cooking during the holidays, it was comparable to missing a meeting with the

> Isn't it amazing that if God tells us about all the wonderful promises He has for us, we still ask for physical proof before we believe Him?

President of the United States. That's just how remarkable her meals were.

My wife, daughter and I decided to go over to my grandmother's house on the 4th of July of 2010. This particular holiday will always remain in the forefront of my mind. A lot had changed. I had been married four years, had a beautiful and energetic two-year-old daughter, and had been involved in ministry and motivational speaking for seven years. However, I felt a bit of uneasiness each passing day. It was my two-year-old daughter who helped me to quickly identify what caused me to feel sullen and gloomy most days.

---

[9] 2 Corinthians 5:17, New King James Version.

On this particular day my daughter woke up around 7:00 a.m. and ran into our room, jumped up and down in the middle of our bed and yelled with excitement and joy, "I want pool mamma. I want pool daddy." My wife and I had told her we were going to take her to the pool the night before. She had developed a fondness for the water at her daycare. Sometimes they set up sprinkler water games and allowed her class to dress up in swimwear outfits and enjoy the water. Continuing to jump up and down, I noticed my daughter's eyes light up in anticipation. It was amazing she had not forgotten our promise from the night before. Since this 4th of July fell on a Sunday, my wife and I explained to our daughter that we would go to church first and then take her to the pool around 3 o'clock.

If you know anything about two year olds, then you know that when they want their way they throw these really big temper tantrums. She let us have it. "I want pool Mamma! I want pool Daddy!" She yelled as if nothing in the world, not even our voices, would stop her. After leaving church, we rushed home so we could grab our swimming items. We packed our swimwear and dressed our daughter in her bathing suit.

She was so excited that she even asked my wife to put on her favorite "Dora-the-Explorer" glasses, a gift from her second birthday. Envision our daughter as she walked with us out of the door: a bathing suit, a radiant smile, sunglasses, a float on her right arm and a towel on her left arm.

After the short drive, we finally arrived at my grandmother's home. Immediately my daughter yelled, "Pool Mamma, I want pool!" We were not yet in the house, but still she yelled for the pool. Looking back, I understand how important it is to have child-like faith and determination. Before we could get into the house, she again started kicking and screaming about going swimming again. We hadn't spoken to anyone, joined the family for dinner, or socialized at all. The thing that amazed me about my daughter's eagerness is that she never saw the pool. She had only heard about it.

It was her faith that garnered my attention. Isn't it amazing that if God tells us about all the wonderful promises He has for us, we still ask for physical proof before we believe Him? We readily allow our beliefs to be controlled by what we see versus what God has promised. We quickly allow others to diminish our faith, passion, and pursuit of that which is before us. We must not shy away from what we desire, or what we have yet to see.

No voices by the pool

My nephew, two years older than my daughter, had come over to my grandmother's house as well. My daughter loves to be around him when she has the chance. While my wife and I greeted family and socialized, my daughter saw my nephew's swim attire. Boy, did that encourage her more! This caused her to believe even more that water was somewhere near. Before you knew it, both of them started yelling with excitement, "Pool, we want pool!"

87

At that point we knew it was time to go ahead and allow them to enjoy the water. Little did my daughter and nephew know it, but they were teaching me how important it is to have someone you can identify with, who desires the same destination that you do. I mentioned earlier that it is dangerous to travel life's road alone. It is easier for the enemy to send voices contrary to your destination to derail you from arriving at your destiny or purpose.

Even Solomon echoed this sentiment in Ecclesiastes 4:9-10: *"Two are better than one, Because they have a good reward for their labor; for if they fall, one will lift up his companion. But woe to him who is alone when he falls, for he has no one to help him up."*[10]

There are tremendous benefits in walking with someone rather than living in isolation. My daughter and nephew exemplified this school of thought at a very young age. They grabbed every adult they could find to take them to the pool. My grandmother's house has a beautiful back yard that slopes in a hill. Toward the bottom are beautiful flowerbeds, lush green grass, steps that lead up to the top of the hill with a concrete sitting area and a pool. As we walked toward the pool, in the back of my mind I knew I did not really want to go swimming. My plans were to sit on the edge and hold my daughter as she splashed in the water. Suddenly as we made it to the side of the pool, my daughter tugged and pulled away from my wife's hand and started running for the

---

[10] Ecclesiastes 4:9-10, New King James Version.

water. It shocked us both: luckily we caught her before she got a chance to jump in and possibly drown.

She was only two years old with no actual swimming experience. What would make her fearlessly pursue something that could be dangerous for her? As we stopped my daughter, my wife turned to me and said, "Man, she really does not have any fear!" At that moment, my daughter's action brought such clarity of how "stuck" I had become in my thinking and reasoning, my faith in God, and my ability to dream without fear.

I'll never forget my wife's words, "That was the first time in almost two years the empty feeling connected with a practical example." At that moment, I finally understood the fear I had collected over the years by listening to people tell me what I couldn't do. I had accepted counterproductive criticism based on their life experiences rather than sound counsel. All of that created the self-doubting voices that I had grown accustomed to hearing in my head.

After coming to grips with years of negative thoughts of conviction, I decided to get in the pool with my daughter. In a mere second, she taught me how to destroy fear, doubt, and the mental barriers. She taught me how to *not* listen. Her actions, although dangerous, showed me the importance of how and to whom we listen. We stayed in the pool for hours. I walked back and forth in the shallow end of the pool holding her in my arms as she got a kick out of splashing in the water.

Her dream of being in the water had come true because she chose to hold on to our promise. She didn't listen to weather reports, her mom and dad telling her to wait, or our family members picking her up admiring how much she had grown and how pretty she had gotten. She only had one thing in mind— swimming. She only listened to the voice of desire and possibility—and nothing else! She screamed joyously, splashed, and kicked in the water until her little heart was content. The entire time in the water I kept asking myself, "Why wasn't she scared to run toward the pool without anyone to protect her?" I could conclude only that she was not listening to voices telling her she couldn't. Innocence and desire gave her the freedom to live carefree without limits. How do I know this? I soon learned another lesson.

Shortly after we got into the pool, more of my younger cousins came up and began swimming with us. They were pre-teens and teenagers, so they were advanced swimmers. Most of them had taken swimming lessons before and probably had been swimming for years. My daughter got a kick at watching them swim and splash water at each other. She splashed right along with them. We were still all on the shallow end. Finally, my cousins decided to stop splashing water and approached the deeper end of the pool. They began jumping off the diving board, doing cannon balls, dives, and silly jumps. My daughter watched them intently and was excited about seeing them jump from the diving board; she began saying, "Daddy, I don't want pool!" It was funny

90

because what she was actually trying to communicate that she wanted to get out and try to jump from the driving board. She believed she could do it too! She started kicking and screaming until I let her get out and stand on the edge with my wife. "Momma, Daddy, I'll be back!" she yelled and she started running toward the diving board. Again, we had to catch her and explain to her why she couldn't dive yet. We explained that she could enjoy this pool fun at another time in the future. Thankfully, this time she agreed and watched them from the side.

What will you do?

My questions to you are simple but critical. What voices have gotten you stuck? What thoughts do you permit to create paralyzing moments in your life? It is critical because you could be making damaging decisions, not reaching your potential, not moving forward, or framing your entire world around a falsehood. Of course the list that I mentioned earlier is not exhaustive. The point is to recognize the voices attached to your thought process. Now is the time to stop telling yourself, "I can't … I'll always be in this position … Nobody likes me … I'll never overcome what they said about me …"

I urge you to identify those voices and learn to cast them down (do not believe them), discard them, challenge them, and fight them with faith and God's truth. You will need to replace false thoughts with new thoughts, and you do that by the content you take in. Learn to replace old content with content that contains truth and will speak to your future. The four leprous men had to leave their past behind them (including all the negativity they heard about their leprosy) in order to build up enough faith to move forward. It would have been tragic if they had never moved forward because of what they heard in their past. Are voices from your past holding you back? Well, here is great relief—God desires that you listen to His truth over the lies you have believed about yourself from the enemy and negative people. I challenge you to discard those negative voices and follow His voice (in His Word).

Getting Past Stuck
CHECK UP

Points to ponder

1. What we listen to shapes our thoughts, personality, fears, and the direction we travel.

2. We must overcome any negatives voices from our past and present.

3. God knows all truth about who we are and what we will become. We must believe His voice.

4. Identify the voice you have struggled with and overcome it by feeding yourself God's truth.

5. Do not believe the enemy's lies. Not only are they infectious, they are damaging.

6. God can do the impossible in your life if you believe what He believes about you.

7. Take a leap of extreme faith. Doing this builds up your trust in God. Trusting Him will help you move forward.

Focus Scripture

"Do not remember the former things, Nor consider the things of old. Behold, I will do a new thing, Now it shall spring forth; Shall you not know it? I will even make a road in the desert."

-Isaiah 43:18-19

Chapter 6

LETTING GOD DRIVE

---

[6] *"...For the LORD had caused the army of the Syrians to hear the noise of chariots and the noise of horses--the noise of a great army..."*

-2 Kings 7:6-8

Life is not a TV series

If people had the option, I'm convinced most would treat their lives like a TV series. The script of their lives would be written to perfection. They would be careful to cover every detail and desire. Every act and scene would be plotted spotlessly, and there probably wouldn't be an antagonist or obstacles opposing their pursuit of happiness. In essence, there wouldn't ever be a pothole in their journey. Unfortunately, life rarely goes exactly according to our plans. In fact, life does not allow us to write the perfect story or decide where, when, and how the plot and scene of our lives will take place. Usually it does not allow an option to avoid any obstacles. Only fairy tales and fictional stories present such a utopian scenario. Although it would be ideal, life is not a TV series. Charles Stanley, in his book, *Living the Extraordinary Life* gives us a transparent look at reality in the twenty-first century. He suggests, "Life in the twenty-first century is rough.

The world is becoming increasingly volatile. Despite the unprecedented technological, scientific, and educational advances, our society grows more fragile with each passing year. Institutional, cultural, and moral foundations upon which we have come to depend are rapidly decaying, and pressures inside and outside the home sometimes overwhelm us."[1] In a nutshell, he is suggesting that life has no perfect conditions. There is only a perfect God who desires to divinely orchestrate the plans of our lives. Inevitably, our plans will be redirected or altered by circumstances or poor decisions; especially when our plan(s) do not align with God's will for our life. We must be careful of trying to pen the script of our lives apart from God, or inviting God to ride in our "vehicle of life" and politely asking him to ride in the backseat. That's how most of our lives get stuck—not allowing him to drive in the beginning. We would avoid many dead ends we run into if we allowed him to just take the wheel and drive.

The leprous men were placed outside of their home camp, and suffered a life-threatening condition (leprosy) for trying to take life in their own hands. How? Because leprosy in the Old Testament came as a result of persons violating the law of God. Only when they released control and decided to surrender did they become recipients of God's grace. Am I saying not to think? Of course not. I'm simply saying that if we try to control every aspect of our lives—we'll end up frustrated and disappointed. There are

---

[1] Charles F. Stanley. *Living the Extraordinary Life*. (Nashville, TN: Thomas Nelson, 2005), xi.

just some things in life that we cannot control. Have you tried to write the perfect script apart from God? Let me save you some time, it does not work. Have you even thought God was leading you to do something and He wasn't? Sometimes, trying to order our own steps holds us back. Sure, we mean well, but the end result is deep disappointment.

Writing a script without God

My wife and I heard a story about a single young woman who desperately wanted to get married. In her opinion, she had found the perfect man. Her plans were to finish school, work in her desired career field, and have a flawless marriage without God at the center of their marriage or dating. At the time we heard this story, my wife and I were not yet married; it was more of a passing thought than a concrete idea. During this young woman's planning of her wedding, we were told of how she planned for a picture perfect wedding including a beautiful dress and décor. Not once did she ever mention God in her plans (or whether her future mate was grounded in the Lord). We heard that she explained how magnificently prepared the reception would be and how many people would come out and support them on this day. Occasionally, we heard that she would even go out of her way to let people know how much it was going to cost to execute all of her elaborate plans.

The young woman had become more concerned with what the wedding would look like than with the work of making a marriage healthy or basing the marriage upon a Christ-centered relationship. She looked at what would take place as a TV series. She had the perfect script in her mind; she would have the perfect house, the right career, and most of all, the man she wanted. She was almost right with everything she planned. The wedding was a success with many guests who came out to wish the couple well. It was indeed a beautiful day! The event cost a lot (tens of thousands of dollars), but their marriage lasted less than a year. Time revealed

> We must be cognizant that our lives can take a turn at any moment, without our consent or control.

that the husband was violent, he cheated, and she was left in emotional shambles. Nearly five years later, she still has not fully recovered. The young woman eventually started to sleep around with other men to cover up her internal pain. The unexpected happened in her life and left her questioning herself and her faith in God. Her perfect script was destroyed. She quickly found out that life is not perfect and does not always go according to how we plan it. This is particularly true when we plan our lives apart from God, wise counsel, and wisdom. We quickly see that He is a better driver and scriptwriter than we will ever be. This experience did tons to the young woman's thought process. She now lives her life based upon the emotional abuse she suffered. Isn't it amazing how one wrong decision apart from God can cause us emotional hurt, frustration, and time wasted? We are now praying that she gets past this rough patch.

God is in total control

Proverbs 16:9 says, *"We plan the way we want to live, but only God makes us able to live it."*[2] We can plan that all of our proverbial ducks will be lined in a row, or that we will have the best job with ideal pay after college, and end up working in a career field we least expect. We can tell ourselves we will be in a certain place based upon our personal goals, or retire by a certain age, and situations occur where we are delayed in our goals or laid off ten years before we planned to retire. We must be cognizant that our lives can take a turn at any moment, without our consent or control. We could even plan to train our children with respect and dignity and somehow they choose to go the opposite direction from what we hope and expect. Unexpected events surround us, and the more we plan for the perfect setting, flawless performances, and strategic planning the further away from the mark we land. That's why we must place all flats in God's hands and allow Him to work out every unexpected event or tragedy that occurs in our life. The scripture is very definitive in letting us know that life can give us back something we never asked for, and the grand scheme of life is ultimately up to God.

Don't blame God

In fact, when life does not go as expected, God is often blamed first. We move beyond our comprehension of life, and question Him as to say, "If you are so in control, why can't I have my way?"

---

[2] Proverbs 16:9, The Message Version.

The young woman's marriage ended tragically—just like many other tragic stories. Sadly, she cut off all communication with many people who previously supported her. Most importantly, she alienated herself from God. She became enraged and felt that somehow God was behind her failed marriage and that He was holding her back. She was in a place where most people find themselves and failed to admit it. She was "stuck!" She began living a life of routine existence rather than a life of purpose. She held onto her script instead of balling it up, throwing it into the trash, and asking God to give her His script for her life. Misery quickly became her constant companion. She was mad at God, but she desperately needed His help.

STUCK without God's plans

As each passing day goes by, more and more people continue to make the most important plans of their lives, writing beautiful scripts, setting the scene(s), but not including God as the director. They continue to make plans without seeking God's

> Blaming is the easiest thing to do when we can't control what's happening in our lives.

advice. They blame Him when things deviate from their plans. Many people get mad at God when they haven't felt His anthropomorphic hand move for a while. Others turn away because in their limited perception they feel they have never seen it move at all. Really, they just haven't been paying attention or they are too spiritually immature to recognize His presence and methods. It is true that before God can help us, we must invite Him to intervene in our lives. He does not force Himself on anyone. The Bible teaches in Revelation 3:20, *"Behold, I stand at the door and knock. If anyone hears My voice and opens the door, I will come in to him and dine with him, and he with Me."*[3] God literally wants to help and aid us in any way possible. He does wait for an invitation.

Many people get stuck because they focus on the negatives. They get "stuck" because they grow comfortable blaming God and everything around them. As stated in an earlier chapter, blaming is the easiest thing to do when we can't control what's happening in our lives. God wants us to leave everything in the boat and trust Him more. We must not be mad at God. Rather, we should yield and work *with* Him. When Jesus called Peter to come walk on the water in Matthew, Chapter 14, He didn't tell him to bring designer luggage or past relationship problems. He simply uttered the command to "Come." I've learned over the years that we get mad at God when we are impatient. We get mad at Him when things are really frustrating and there is no quick answer.

When we get mad at God, we literally stop praying or trying to draw close to Him. Additionally, we are prone to stop reading His word, and slowly drift away because we are mad. We take the disposition, "If He hasn't done anything for me yet, why should I continue to call out to Him?" Let me quickly tell you that feeling like this can damage our hope. One thing we should never do while we are feeling "stuck" is blame God. He never wants to

---

[3] Revelations 3:20, New King James Version.

hurt us; He only wants to help us. In Jeremiah 29:11 we find very familiar words, *"For I know the thoughts that I think toward you, says the LORD, thoughts of peace and not of evil, to give you a future and a hope."*[4]

It's when we want life to move at our every command at the instant we snap our fingers that we lose our bearings. We want life to move at our pace and give us what we desire—right NOW! Why? Because we are set on our plans, not His plans for our lives. God wants an unconditional commitment to Him (even when He is testing us).

Does God approve?

To be honest, the most dangerous thing to do is to live life outside the will of God and not even ask Him if He approves of your plans, or see if your plans align with His word. There is a parable in the Gospels that illustrates the point. It takes place as Jesus travels from city to city preaching and teaching in small villages, synagogues, and houses about the Kingdom of God. A young man approaches Jesus. This young man is identified as the rich young ruler. Obviously, this young man was wealthy, in charge of a large number of people, and had kept the Levitical laws issued to the children of Israel by Moses. It would appear that this young man was a great success. However, something was missing inside. He approached Jesus and began to dialogue with Him. It was obvious this young man had established his life around doing good things and planning good things to please himself. He was

---

[4] Jeremiah 29:11, New King James Version.

like me as I stated earlier—living life with meaningless works alone. He gives himself away by calling Jesus "good." Let's recount the story.

"Now a certain ruler asked Him, saying, "Good Teacher, what shall I do to inherit eternal life?" So Jesus said to him, "Why do you call Me good? No one is good but One, that is, God. You know the commandments:

'Do not commit adultery,' 'Do not murder,' 'Do not steal,' 'Do not bear false witness,' 'Honor your father and your mother.'" And he said, "All these things I have kept from my youth." So when Jesus heard these things, He said to him, "You still lack one thing. Sell all that you have and distribute to the poor, and you will have treasure in heaven; and come, follow Me." But when he heard this, he became very sorrowful, for he was very rich."[5]

> It is amazing how our plans can become a false god or idol to us if we are not careful.

Many scholars, theologians, pastors, and teachers have overemphasized that this young man's downfall was his unwillingness to let go of his money. Although they are right, I believe this young man had fallen victim to what the everyday person in Western Culture does on a daily basis—living and planning their entire lives without God actually being first. We want the perfect script and want to please ourselves so much we

---

[5] Luke 18:18-23, New King James Version.

subconsciously push God out of the picture and replace Him with our performance and desires.

In the passage, the young man asks Jesus what might He do to be saved, and justifies himself by telling Jesus how good he has been by keeping all of the commandments. This young man was surely shocked to hear Jesus say to him in so many words you have put your plans in front of God. Inevitably, this is why the young man walks away with a sorrowful disposition—he not only loved money more than God, but the plans for his life were more important. It is amazing how our plans can become a false god or idol to us if we are not careful. In his book, *The Counterfeit God*, Timothy Keller addresses idolatry among God's people and those things that rob our hearts from truly experiencing God as the first priority in our lives.

"A counterfeit god is anything so central and essential to your life that, should you lose it, your life would feel hardly worth living. An idol has such a controlling position in your heart that you can spend most of your passion, energy, and your emotional and financial resources on it without a second thought. It can be family and children, or career and making money, or achievement and critical acclaim, or saving 'face' and social standing. It can be a romantic relationship, peer approval, competence and skill, secure and comfortable circumstances, your beauty or your brains, a great political or social cause, your morality and virtue, or even success in the Christian ministry."[6]

We are okay with God until He requires from us the very thing that has our heart more than Him. This young man walked away "stuck" because he refused to let go of his personal plans. Have you come to a point where you acknowledge you have made decisions without God? Or have you been following God's plan for your life but wanted to control it yourself? Whatever the case, you will not get past "stuck" until you release total control of your life to God and surrender. He knows best.

Adopting God's plans more than our own

One of my favorite things about reading the Gospels is seeing how each disciple was chosen by Jesus, and how they forsook all they had known to follow Him. In Matthew, 9:9 we find the disciple Matthew called by Jesus to forsake his thriving business and follow Christ. *"As Jesus passed on from there, He saw a man named Matthew sitting at the tax office. And He said to him, "Follow Me." So he arose and followed Him."*[7] What impresses me most about Matthew is that he had achieved success and made a lot of money and probably had every possible plan unfold just as planned. Yet he gave it all up because he felt the call and plans of God were more important than his own. It never said that Matthew complained about how well he was doing without Christ, or how he had to close his business for the day and let

---

[6] Timothy Keller. *Counterfeit Gods*. (New York, NY: Penguin Group, 2009), xviii.

[7] Matthew 9:9, New King James Version.

everybody know he was going to be gone for a couple of days and would return.

Using my imagination in a modern day scenario, I picture Matthew going into work that day, saying to himself that it was going to be another great day, just like he planned it would be. He was probably patting himself on the back for being so successful. He also probably checked his list of priorities and possibly gave some of his workers assigned duties for the day. Suddenly, Jesus walked by and says, "Hey Matthew, I see something greater in you, and God's plans for your life are better than where you are. Would you follow me?" Without hesitation, Matthew probably dropped the to-do list, hung up the telephone, and walked straight out of the door without letting a single soul know. He gave it all up to follow Christ. How great it would be if we stopped everything in our lives to follow God's Son and His plans for our lives. Another large part of getting past "stuck" is forsaking our personal plans for God's divine plans. We take our plans and toss them in the trash. That's what I did. I took everything I used to create love in my life and tossed it for God's love.

We do not want to be like the disciple in the Book of Matthew, Chapter 8, who makes excuses to Jesus when asked to follow Him, *"Then a certain scribe came and said to Him, 'Teacher, I will follow You wherever You go.' And Jesus said to him, 'Foxes have holes and birds of the air have nests, but the Son of Man has nowhere to lay His head.' Then another of His disciples said to Him, 'Lord, let me first go and bury my father.'*

But Jesus said to him, 'Follow Me, and let the dead bury their own dead.'"[8] The second disciple gave a to-do list before committing fully to follow Jesus.

Stop, Pray, Ask

If you have been putting your plans before God's, I challenge you to stop, pray, and ask God what he requires of you. God longs to work out every detail of your life, but He can't until you surrender totally to Him. You must ask yourself—Is God planning my life, or am I? When we looked at the story of the four lepers, we quickly see that it wasn't until they let go of their plans and surrendered that God's grace was able to magnify their footsteps and scare away their enemies. *"For the LORD had caused the army of the Syrians to hear the noise of chariots and the noise of horses—the noise of a great army; so they said to one another, 'Look, the king of Israel has hired against us the kings of the Hittites and the kings of the Egyptians to attack us!' Therefore they arose and fled at twilight, and left the camp intact—their tents, their horses, and their donkeys—and they fled for their lives. And when these lepers came to the outskirts of the camp, they went into one tent and ate and drank, and carried from it silver and gold and clothing, and went and hid them; then they came back and entered another tent, and carried some from there also, and went and hid it."*[9] Take a moment to pray and ask God to confirm His direction

---

[8] Matthew 8:19-22, New King James Version.
[9] 2 Kings 7:6-8, New King James Version.

for your life. If you do not know what to say, I have included a prayer for direction.

Prayer for God's direction

Dear Lord,

For so long I have tried to live my life the way that I have wanted apart from your will. There have even been times where I have tried to live by your will, but still wanted to maintain total control of my life. Now, I feel totally lost. I'm hurt, I'm confused, and I'm in need of you to take over. Please reveal your will for my life and order my steps completely. Help me to overcome any bad decision(s) I have made, or anything I still hold against you or myself. I desire to live my life according to your plans. Lord, I open my heart, mind, and spirit to you. I humbly ask you to direct my life. Connect me with those who will help counsel me to the next phase of my life and pull out the best in me. Teach me how to draw closer to you Lord and be more discerning. Add meaningful, healthy, and stable relationships to my life. Lord, have your way in my heart.

If you have not accepted Jesus, I encourage you to say this simple prayer. *Lord, I believe that you are God, and that Jesus is your Son. I believe your son was buried and resurrected for my sins. I accept him as Lord and Savior of my life.* From here I encourage you to get plugged into a local church. If you have already received Christ, I challenge you to allow God to renew, revive, and refresh your faith.

Getting Past Stuck
CHECK UP

Points to ponder

1. We do not have the power or foreknowledge to write the script of our life; only God does.
2. Our plans fail when they are not aligned with God's will for our life.
3. We must not blame God for our failed plans, especially when they were made apart from Him.
4. We must not allow our personal plans to become an idol or god to us.
5. We must always balance our plans with God's truth.
6. God has a powerful plan for your life. Just because you have experienced loss, tragedy, or heartache does not mean that He is through with you.
7. Never be scared to abandon your prospering plans for Jesus.
8. Take time to stop, pray, and ask God for direction.

Focus Scripture

"But what things were gain to me, these I have counted for loss for Christ. Yet indeed I also count all things loss for the excellence of the knowledge of Christ Jesus my Lord, for whom I have suffered

the loss of all things, and count them as rubbish, that I may gain

Christ."

-Philippians 3:7-8

Chapter 7

THANKING GOD FOR SPARES

---

[9] *"Then they said to one another, "We are not doing right. This day* is *a day of good news, and we remain silent..."*

-2 Kings 7:8-9

Being stuck is hardly new. History records countless episodes. The one thing about getting past stuck is that you have the power and testimony to share the good news of what God has done in your life after you start moving forward from where you are. The four leprous men knew this truth. They discussed this important truth right after God performed one of the biggest miracles of their lives. They had this simple conversation: *"Then they said to one another, "We are not doing right. This day* is *a day of good news, and we remain silent. If we wait until morning light, some punishment will come upon us. Now therefore, come, let us go and tell the king's household."*[1] They simply learned to be grateful for the small things and then determined to share that gratitude with the king's household. The funny thing about being stuck is that sometimes we are not stuck at all. We are simply where God wants us so that He can reveal to us who is ultimately

---

[1] 2 Kings 7:9, New King James Version.

in control. Additionally, it is just a conscious choice to live in the *now* and let go of the past and future. Sure, we make bad decisions and choices, but He is still working out the fabric of our lives.

We will now turn to some modern-day stories that have impacted my life personally. I love looking at how God works in the lives of those around me and in the world at large. Sometimes, looking at how God has worked out details in someone else's life builds faith in us. These are stories in which God took the absolute worst and used it for absolute good. It is *true* that God sends spare(s) to help us move forward in the midst of our "stuckness." That's what He did in the lives of the lepers, what He did in the lives of the modern examples and stories all around us, and what He will do for you. God essentially caused each of these people to "Get Past Stuck."

> Sometimes, looking at how God has worked out details in someone else's life builds faith in us.

The Story of Alfred Bernhard Nobel

Alfred Bernhard Nobel found himself in a position to go down in history. In error, the local newspapers had printed his obituary rather than that of his deceased brother. This error allowed him to see how he would have been perceived had he actually died. Years earlier, Alfred Nobel had invented dynamite. His motives in doing so were honorable because he saw it as a way to build roads, tunnel through rocks and a number of other positive uses. He became very wealthy from this invention. In addition to the invention of dynamite, he is credited with over 350 patents for various other inventions. When Nobel's brother died, a newspaper picked up the story and thought that it was the same man who invented dynamite. By then the substance had many uses, including a weapon of mass destruction and death in wars.

Consequently, this man who loved peace, poetry and the most beautiful things in life was mistakenly labeled as a kind of "Dr. Death" in the obituary. It saddened Nobel to see what the world could have really thought of him if he had indeed died at that point. Yet it was good that he had the chance to see how he might be remembered. Fortunately, he was alive and free to alter this very negative set of circumstances. He decided that he would not leave this world with such an unfortunate and distorted reputation. He had time to make a difference! Nobel then decided to pledge his wealth to a prestigious award in the name of peace— NOT WAR!

First, he established a foundation that would identify outstanding world recipients with an award in chemistry, medicine, physics, literature and efforts toward international peace. As a result of his determination not to be "stuck" with a negative and destructive legacy, his name is associated with great contributions and superb humanitarian efforts. The Nobel Prize is one of the most prestigious awards in the world. In addition to the honor of being selected as the winner of the award, Nobel's wealthy estate provides a large cash gift. Now, rather than being known as one of the world's mongers of destruction and death, Alfred Nobel's name rings ceremoniously each year as one the world's greatest humanitarians. Many individuals are now aligned with this great man. He chose not to be "stuck" with a soiled legacy and has unselfishly brought the names of many individuals before the entire world. The Nobel Foundation, based in Sweden, has recognized many individuals from the year 1901 until today. As the annual announcements are made each year, people remember Alfred Nobel as a great man of tremendous achievement. God did turn his entire situation around through the power of one thought.

The Story of Dr. Ben Carson, MD Pediatric Neurosurgeon

Dr. Ben Carson's rise to prominence was, by most standards, fairly unpredictable. He grew up in the home of a single mother who worked very hard to raise a family alone. Each day she left their home and sent her sons to school, hoping that one day they might succeed and never be forced to do the kind of jobs she had to do. They lived in Detroit, Michigan, where many young people fell by the wayside and lived out the unfortunate expectancy of society—to be troublemakers who contributed little to the community. In retrospect, Carson admits now that he did little to help himself and used his charismatic personality to perform as the class clown. Acting out was fun and easier than buckling down and doing his schoolwork. Even though he was quite intelligent, his grades were awful. He loved the attention he received from his antics.

Sonya Carson, his mother, did not give up on her dreams for him and his brother. She required both sons to read two books each week and write book reports, which they then turned in to her.

Many years later, Dr. Carson found out that his mother could not read at all. She had left school in the third grade. Each week she collected the book reports, knowing that they would add to her children's overall development; she knew full well the advantage of being able to read, interpret and apply written information. She worked two or three jobs at a time to keep her household going. She had very little money and few resources for help, yet she recognized the power of a well-trained mind.

Though society might have written him off, there were other people who did not give up on Dr. Carson. Recognizing great potential, some of his teachers continued to challenge him until he made a change and re-channeled his energy. The story goes that one day while in class, one of Dr. Carson's teachers asked a question about a particular kind of rock. Instead of thinking of something funny to say to make the class laugh, Dr. Carson remembered a book that he had read before submitting the usual book report to his mother. He knew the exact answer to the question and really surprised the teacher. In fact, he went on to share other information about other rocks, much to the astonishment of a teacher who had grown used to his usual behavior. The teacher was impressed! More importantly, Dr. Carson was impressed with HIMSELF!

He graduated from high school and entered Yale University. By this time his head was indeed on straight. He studied hard and did extremely well. His mother could now boast that her son was well on the way to becoming a doctor. Carson was at the same time gaining the admiration of his professors and fellow students. He finished medical school and interned in Pediatric Neurosurgery. For an adult male, he had exceptionally thin and agile fingers, which equipped him to function in this particular area. Neurosurgery on small infants was a very delicate task. It seemed as though his hands were made for such intricate tasks. At the age of 32, he became Director of Pediatric Neurosurgery at John Hopkins Children's Hospital in Baltimore, MD.

After he became famous, Dr. Carson released a book called *Gifted Hands*. He toured the United States, inspiring many young people born with humble beginnings to pursue great dreams and never give up. His book became a best seller and many young people credit his story as the one thing that turned them around.

This story could have had a much different ending. Dr. Carson could have dropped out of school, joined a gang and spent the rest of his life doing little good. Without intervention from a determined mother and some of his teachers, he might have destroyed lives rather than saved them. Instead, he will go down in history as the gifted African American surgeon who successfully performed separation surgery on the Binder Siamese twins. Two tiny infants, connected at birth, were given a chance at living a normal life after going under the scalpel of this former class clown who decided that he did not have to be stuck in the mire of low expectations and low productivity. The now famous surgery involved a surgical team of seventy persons and took approximately twenty-two hours.

Carson could have looked out the window at the boys on the corner, the drugs in the street and the gang messages on the walls of buildings. In fact, he probably took a look at all of these things and decided that he could do much better. Even though he was known as a "cut-up" in his early school years, he was smart enough to know that all of this activity would leave him stuck in this community (or even worse) for the rest of his life. He did love his mother and appreciated her hard work and struggle. He wanted something better for both of them. Dr. Carson decided NOT TO BE STUCK!

THE MIRACLE IN CHILE: Thirty-three Vivid Examples of Moving Beyond "Stuck"

Many lessons gleaned are from the miracle which occurred in Copiapo, Chile during the summer of 2010. It was here that a monumental copper mine cave-in commanded the world's attention. Thirty-three men were trapped more than 2300 feet beneath the earth's surface. The news rapidly traveled around the world. Many felt there was no way that this saga could end well. Firstly, no one, except the entombed miners, knew exactly where they were. Secondly, they were so deep within the earth that it seemed impossible to be able to locate, reach and save them in time. Thirdly, by all human calculations, there was not enough food, air or water in the mine to support survival of thirty-three individuals for more than just a few days.

It took over seventeen days of trial and error to pinpoint their location. Yet much to the surprise of an expert team of rescuers, they were all still alive! Realizing that they were "stuck" unless they took authority over their life-challenging situation, the miners resolved to participate in their own preservation.

Surveying the possible outcomes of the situation, experts speculated that ultimately, survival depended upon the miners themselves in a number of ways. Firstly, they needed to **share the faith** that they could overcome this confinement. Secondly, they needed to **identify and respect leadership.** Thirdly, each individual needed to **participate wholeheartedly** in their own rescue without selfish regard to their own needs.

Imagine the potential for chaos in this situation. Immediately following the incident, the mine shaft was filled with smoke, temporarily blinding the miners for nearly six hours— thirty-three blinded men in an enclosed, hot and humid space. Fortunately, the dust finally settled and they could see faintly in the dark enclosure. They began to try to find a way of escape through ventilation shafts; however, contrary to mining rules, there were no ladders. As they looked at the situation they once again agreed that they were quite—STUCK! On the ground's surface, it had already been broadcast around the world that the destiny of the men lay somewhere between God and the leadership skills and positive interaction of the men. The men were destined to play a key role in their own destiny.

The shift supervisor then took control and began to design a makeshift relief plan. The men with the greatest number of years and experience in mining were assigned to survey the cave-in and possible plans for escape. Other men with very specific skills were assigned very specific duties. In the meantime, the people on the earth's surface as well as the trapped miners were handicapped by outdated maps that should have been redrawn years earlier. It seemed as though their case of being "STUCK" was compounded with every fleeting moment. If that wasn't bad enough, the experts agreed that it would take *months* to reach them safely. They faced a slow and treacherous rescue attempt. The wrong move could initiate another cave-in, resulting in the certain death of the waiting workers.

The miners were confined in a very small area (approximately 540 square feet). Under the leadership of the foremen, the following decisions were made:

1. To use backhoes in the shaft to dig for underground water.
2. To drain water from the radiators of mining vehicles they were using at the time of the incident.
3. To ration an emergency two to three day food supply for distribution every forty-eight hours (This amounted to two teaspoons of tuna and a sip of milk).
4. To use battery energy from the mining trucks to power battery-operated hard hats.
5. To organize the confinement area into spaces for the following needs—medical supplies, safety needs, and storage.

6. To provide special provision for the oldest miner (age sixty-three) who had pre-existing health issues.

7. To use a natural waterfall adjacent to the area of confinement for a shower source.

8. To regularly sing the Chilean anthem as a symbol of their ongoing interdependence and determination.

By now this did not look like a scene where individuals were planning to die. It reminds me of the lepers who made a similar decision.

"ESTAMOS BIEN EN EL REFUGIO LOS 33"

On August 17, over two weeks after the incident, a drill bit was returned to the rescue surface. Attached to the drill was a crude note written with a red marker by one of the miners:

"ESTAMOS BIEN EN EL REFUGIO LOS 33" Translation: "We are all right in the shelter, the 33 [of us]." As the men acted in faith, it was indeed possible to escape being "STUCK." The rescuers on the surface also implemented a plan. Scientists and experts from at least four countries came together to perform a modern-day miracle. As a result, the following above-ground operations took place: 1) The rescue team provided daily consultations and briefings using video and audio transmission to the foreman. 2) The team included a physician, a psychologist and an experienced miner. 3) Medical supplies were lowered into the same tube. They were dispensed by the one miner who had some medical training. It was also his job to perform tests, chart the medical condition of each individual, and administer medication.

He especially noted any noticeable health changes. 4) Written messages were received on the surface from the miners through the tube. This allowed them to communicate with their families and loved ones. This helped to dispel the torture of loneliness and isolation.

Faith plays a key role

With one exception, all of the miners were from Chile. The non-Chilean miner was from Bolivia. Both countries are predominantly Catholic. Both countries are fairly religious. As soon as the miners were contacted by the outside world, they began to request Bibles and other religious artifacts.

> When you think that you cannot move forward, always remember the story of the miracle in Chile.

International broadcasts revealed groups of people at the site of the rescue singing, praying and praising God for a miracle. The Pope, recognized as the supreme spiritual leader of the Catholic Church, sent rosaries for each trapped individual. In the midst of being "STUCK," the captives were reminded that a higher power oversaw their fate. The foreman designated the oldest miner (the one with respiratory health issues) as the spiritual leader of the group. He had previously faced many challenges that required faith, perseverance and wisdom. As a result, the men set up a makeshift chapel so that while off duty from a mandatory eight-hour shift, they could pray, receive counsel and continue to petition God for deliverance.

Initially, for the sake of their emotional stability, the rescuers did not tell the miners that they anticipated that their rescue was months away. They felt this bit of news could harm the prevailing calm and peace. As their faith and tenacity increased, they were eventually made aware of the timeline and accepted the information with reasonable resolve and even more determination to help to make it happen!

Finally, after sixty-eight days of confinement, the first miner was brought to the surface. In honor and tribute, he FIRST fell on his knees, prayed, and lifted his hands toward heaven in gratitude to a God who, once again, had engineered a miracle! Only after he did this did he look for his family and loved ones who embraced him in sheer delight. It took approximately two additional days to rescue the other miners—one by one! The foreman was the last to emerge from a tomb that no longer held inhabitants. Once again, death and doubt had suffered defeat! The world jubilantly celebrated this conquest.

This story is one of the most descriptive templates that I can offer. The story illustrates that release and freedom from the mud of life can be attained by the following plan:

THE PLAN

1. **Acceptance** of the fact that you are temporarily in a "STUCK" position.
2. **Submission** to leadership of individuals designated to provide help and instruction.

3. **Willingness to work with others** to benefit your needs as well as the needs of others.

4. **Personal sharing** of God-given talents and gifts.

5. **Reliance** upon God for strength, direction and fortitude to endure.

6. **Commitment** to a life of prayer and spiritual growth even in dark times.

7. **Faith** in spite of how things look.

8. **Gratitude** after God brings you through.

When you think that you cannot move forward, always remember the story of the miracle in Chile and the magnificent example of becoming free! As you recount the details of the episode, I hope that you will agree there is no sin in becoming temporarily "STUCK." The tragedy occurs only if you remain there! God is more than able to pull you from the mud. Whether you feel as though you have been subjected to a series of emotional flat tires, clinging mud, or a dark and dreadful cave-in, there is hope for you! God in His wisdom, kindness and grace has made a way of escape! He remains in covenant with believers to uphold, protect, provide, and deliver. The lessons of the Chilean disaster remind us of key steps in making sure that we can free ourselves from being "stuck." God can give spares in the midst of chaos and tragedy. He never wants us to be stuck and only plans for us to continuously move forward.

I invite you to reflect upon their journey in order to devise your plan to once again be free. So, you feel you have no idea where to start? I have included a worksheet to help you find your way out of whatever has entangled you! Please fill in the content and reflect on your written work. May God send you a spare in the middle of your wilderness and allow you to "Get Past Stuck."

Best Wishes on your new freedom!

Put in Work!

Getting Past Stuck
CHECK UP

STRATEGIC ACTION PLAN HOMEWORK

---

1. Acceptance of the fact that you are temporarily in a "STUCK" position. There are things in my life that indicate that I'm stuck:
(a)
(b)
(c)

I am now ready to recognize this state of being.
___Not at all
___Somewhat
___Fully

2. Submission to leadership of individuals designated to provide help and instruction. The persons or relationships who serve as potential leaders in my life are:
(a)
(b)
(c)

I will solicit their support in the following way(s):
(a)
(b)
(c)

3. Willingness to work with others to benefit my needs as well as those of others. I understand and appreciate that I am not alone. These are individuals around me who can help me as I help them:
(a)
(b)
(c)

I need help in my life. At the same time I can provide help for others. I can share good news with:
(a)
(b)
(c)

4. Personal sharing of God-given talents and gifts. I can identify the following talents and gifts in my life:
(a)
(b)
(c)

I can start to use my gift in the following way(s):
(a)
(b)
(c)

5.Reliance upon God for strength, direction and fortitude to endure. God is my source and strength. The following scriptures support this truth:
(a)
(b)
(c)

I will use these scriptures in the following way(s) to build or rebuild my faith and the faith of others:
(a)
(b)
(c)

6.Commitment to a life of prayer and spiritual growth even in dark times. I will remain consistent and diligent with my daily walk with God through:

(a)

(b)

(c)

If my faith grows weak, I will read these scriptures and talk to these person(s):

(a)

(b)

(c)

7.Faith in spite of how things look. If I'm not spiritually fortified, the following things could possibly become a source of discouragement:

(a)

(b)

(c)

To counteract any such loss of faith, I will also:

(a)

(b)

(c)

Focus Scripture

"The steps of a good man are ordered by the LORD, and He delights in his way. Though he may fall, he shall not be utterly cast down; For the LORD upholds him with His hand."

-Psalm 37:23-24

Seeking Help

If you feel you need counseling, I suggest that you seek out professionals. There are wonderful people out there whom God has trained to help you get past what has you stuck. However, be cautious in selecting who you counsel with. Make sure they are licensed and have a good history. Although you will have more challenges as you move forward, be reminded of the truth in the scripture, "God will uphold you" if you fall. May God be with you in every step of your journey, and may He cause you to "Get Past Stuck!" God bless you and your family.

Getting Past Stuck
CHECK UP

WELLNESS BOOKS AND COUNSELORS

Many of the books below are literary works that I have read, and the retreats and counseling centers are those that I have researched. They seem to have solid facilities. The book list is very short and not at all a complete list of the wonderful content out there to get you healthy. I simply chose a few of the books that have been meaningful to me. Enjoy.

Books:

- *The Depression Cure* by Stephen S. Ilardi

- *When You've been Wronged* by Erwin W. Lutzer

- *The Wounded Healer* by Henri Nouwen

- *Finding My Way Home* by Henri Nouwen

- *Turning My Mourning into Dancing* by Henri Nouwen

- *The Inner Voice of Love* by Henri Nouwen

- *When People are Big, and God is Small* by Edward Welch

- *Reaching Out* by Henri Nouwen

- *Leading on Empty* by Wayne Cordeiro

- *Freedom of Simplicity* by Richard J. Foster

- *Boundaries* by Henry Cloud and John Townsend

- *Unmasking Male Depression* by Archibald D. Hart.

- *With Open Hands* by Henri Nouwen

- *Where is God when it Hurts* by Phillip Yancey

- *The Reflective Life* by Ken Gire

- *Life of the Beloved* by Henri Nouwen

- *The Return of the Prodigal Son* by Henri Nouwen

Retreats and Counselors (websites):

- www.retreatsonline.com; U.S., Canada, UK, Europe
- www.sonscape.com; CO, GA.
- www.fndthedivine.com/; Over 1,700 retreat centers
- www.parsonage.org
- International Association of Christian Counseling Professionals: www.iaccp.net
- Focus on the Family www.family.org
- American Association of Chistian Counselors Referral Network: www.aacc.net
- National Christian Counselors Association: www.ncca.org

CHAPTER NOTES

Chapter 1

Proverbs 24:10

Bob Phillips. *Controlling Your Emotions Before they Control You*. Eugene, Oregon: Harvest House Publishers, 1995.

William Backus and Marie Chapian. *Telling Yourself the Truth*. Bloomington, Minnesota: Bethany House Publishers, 2000.

Stephen S. Ilardi. *The Depression Cure: The 6-Step Program to Beat Depression Without Drugs*. Cambridge, MA: Da Capo Press, 2009.

Proverbs 23:7

Burton Stokes and Lynn Lucas. *No Longer A Victim*. Shippensburg, PA: Destiny Image Publishers, 1988.

Psalm 19:14

Stephen S. Ilardi. *The Depression Cure: The 6-Step Program to Beat Depression Without Drugs*. Cambridge, MA: Da Capo Press, 2009.

Gerald Corey. *Theory and Practice of Counseling and Psychotherapy*. Eighth Edition. Belmont, CA: Thomas Brooks/Cole, 2009.

Psalm 23:4

Philippians 4:8

Proverbs 13:12

1 Timothy 2:5

Isaiah 40:28-29

Chapter 2

Douglas Stone, Bruce Patton and Sheila Heen. *Difficult Conversations: How to Discuss What Really Matters.* New York, NY: Penguin Group, 1999.

Wayne Cordeiro, *Leading on Empty.* Grand Rapids, MI: Bethany House Publishers, 2009, p. 97.

John C. Maxwell. *Thinking for a Change.* New York, NY: Warner Books, 2003.

Psalm 139:23-24

Proverbs 3:5-6

Proverbs 29:18

2 Kings 6:24

2 Kings 7:3-9

Revelation 12:11

Oswald Chambers. *My Utmost for His Highest: Graduate Edition.* Grand Rapids, Michigan: Discovery House Publishers, 1995.

Unknown Author

Chapter 3

John Mason. *Conquering an Enemy Called Average.* Tulsa, Oklahoma: Insight International, 1996.

Psalm 1:1-3

Henri J. M. Nouwen. *Reaching Out: The Movements Of The Spiritual Life.* New York, NY: Bantam Doubleday Publishing Group, 1975.

Gary R. Collins. *Christian Counseling: A Comprehensive Guide.* W Publishing Group, 1988.

Genesis 2:18

2 Kings 7:3

Proverbs 27:17

Proverbs 13:20

Noel Jones and Georgianna Land. *The Battle for the Mind: How You Can Think the Thoughts of God*. Shippensburg, PA: Destiny Image Publishers, 2006.

1 John 5:14-15

Mark 11:24

Bill Hybels. *Too Busy Not to Pray: Slowing Down to be with God*. Downers Grove, IL: InterVarsity Press, 1998.

Psalm 33:11

Genesis 3:1-10

Chapter 4

2 Corinthians 4:17-18

Hebrews 11:1

James 4:13-17

1 Corinthians 3:6-7

2 Corinthians 12:9

Matthew 5:45

Morris Sheats. *You Can Be Emotionally Healed*. Columbus, GA: Christian Life Publications, 1994.

1 Peter 4:12-13

C. J. Mahaney. *Living the Cross Centered Life: Keeping the Gospel the Main Thing*. Colorado Springs: Multnomah Books, 2006.

Wayne Cordeiro, *Leading on Empty*. Minneapolis: Bethany House Publishers, 2009, 60-64.

Harvard Health Publications (Harvard Medical School). "Dysthymia" This article was first printed in the February 2005 issue of the *Harvard Mental Health Letter*.) Accessed 12 October 2010 available from http://www.health.harvard.edu/newsweek/Dysthymia.htm

1 Corinthians 13:1-13

Chapter 5

2 Timothy 1:7

Romans 12:1-2

Mels Carbonell. *Extreme Personality Makeover: How to Develop a Winning Christ-like Personality to Improve your Effectiveness.* Blue Ridge, GA: Uniquely You Resources, 2005.

John 10:1-10

John Bevere. *How to Respond When You Feel Mistreated.* Nashville, TN: Thomas Nelson Books, 2004.

Edwin Louis Cole. *Maximized Manhood: A Guide to Family Survival.* New Kensington, PA: Whitaker House, 1982.

Ephesians 6:10-20

2 Corinthians 5:17

Ecclesiastes 4:9-10

Chapter 6

Charles F. Stanley. *Living the Extraordinary Life.* Nashville, TN: Thomas Nelson, 2005.

Proverbs 16:9

Revelations 3:20

Jeremiah 29:11

Luke 18:18-23

Timothy Keller. *Counterfeit Gods.* New York, NY: Penguin Group, 2009.

Matthew 9:9

Matthew 8:19-22

2 Kings 7:6-8

Chapter 7

2 Kings 7:9

About the Author

It seems almost unfathomable that Terence Lester sat in a small jail cell eight years ago with sixteen other inmates questioning his life, identity, and direction. Lester was once a juvenile delinquent, high school dropout, suicide attempter, drug user, thief, and gang member. In fact, his story could well have emerged as the recapitulation of another life thrown away. This same story could have easily contributed to growing negative statistics in regards to young men.

However, Lester found a missing piece that has created a beautiful portrait of change. God has caused that piece to change his life—FOREVER! Now, he is on a mission to reach the young and old, lost, confused, hopeless, troubled, and those who might question whether if there is any good in this life for them.

Eight years later, Lester's life looks completely different. He's a family man, author, professor, philanthropist, youth and young adult director, and church planter. Lester has a loving and devoted wife, Cecilia Lester, and two beautiful children Zion Joy and Terence II who support, push, and encourage him on a daily basis. Cecilia's hand is constantly in his work as she upholds and supports his efforts to impact the lives of those he encounters.

From workshops (with college professors, parents, and children), to assemblies, to graduations, to college lectures, to conferences and church services of over 3,000, locally and nationally, Lester has creatively shared his story of change and transformation with relevant language, solid truths, passion, and humor. He has become a much sought-after speaker with hundreds of engagements in elementary, middle and high schools; colleges and universities; many churches; Christian and Non-Christian television; several book festivals; as well as having been featured in several publications.

Lester holds an Associates degree in Media Production, a Bachelor of Theology, a Master of Education, Master of Theological Studies and is currently pursuing his doctorate in Behavioral Sciences. He is the author of four books, and co-producer of a biographical documentary, "The U-Turn Project: Answering The Call." He comes to stand in partnership and agreement with ALL those who love God and are unwilling to give up on the next generation.

Contact Information

Terence Lester is available for speaking engagements, book signings, workshops, and conference participation. Please submit details to the following address:

Terence Lester
PO BOX 1376
Red Oak, GA, 30272

To book engagements, please send the following information:

- Date and length of event and Contact person

- Contact information (phone, fax, email address)

- Event type (conference, church service, youth service, panel participant, etc.)

- Target Audience and Venue (church congregation, mixed ages, youth service, young adults, etc.)

You may go online and request Terence Lester's services or books on the World Wide Web.

Website: www.terencelester.com

Email Address: contact@terencelester.com

Phone: 404-955-8033

Thanks for your support!

www.ingramcontent.com/pod-product-compliance
Lightning Source LLC
Chambersburg PA
CBHW051636050426
42443CB00024B/151